AMAZING
HISTORY

Publications International, Ltd.

Written by:

Mark K. Anderson, Mark W. Anderson, Michael Patrick Brady, Robert Bullington, William W. David, Tom DeMichael, Eric Ethier, Mary Fons Misetic, R.G.W. Griffin, Peter Haugen, Martin Hintz, Jonathan W. Jordan, J.K. Kelley, Jonathan Kelley, David Lesjak, J. David Markham, Rhonda Markowitz, Bill Martin, Michael Martin, Mark McLaughlin, Kimberly Morris, Ed Moser, Richard Mueller, Eric Nelson, Jean Patrick, David Priess, Lawrence Robinson, Bill Sasser, Bryant Smith, Dan Spellerberg, Peter Suciu, James Willis, Chuck Wills

Images by:

Hye Lim An, Art Explosion, Linda Howard Bittner, Erin Burke, Commons.wikimedia.org, Daisy De Puthod, Dan Grant, iStockphoto, Jupiterimages, Nicole H. Lee, Robert Schoolcraft, Shutterstock.com, Shavan R. Spears, Elizabeth Traynor, and John Zielinski

TABLE OF CONTENTS

TABLE OF CONTENTS

TABLE OF CONTENTS

CHAPTER 1
VOYAGES OF DISCOVERY

How Things Really Got Rolling

It's not difficult to see how important the wheel is to human civilization. The hard part is figuring out who got there first.

The wheel is such a simple tool—and yet, determining when it was invented and who did it earliest is anything but simple. Many accounts assert that it was invented in Asia around 8000 B.C. but fail to elaborate.

Our most solid early evidence of the wheel comes from the excavations at the Sumerian city of Ur (in present-day Iraq) and date to about 3500 B.C. We have no idea who invented Sumer's wheel, but we know its function: pottery. One key to civilization is the production of agricultural excess that can be bartered for other goods and services. Without good storage for that excess, varmints will infest it.

The Bronocice Pot, found in Polish digs from the Funnel/Beaker culture, also dates to 3500 B.C. Could the Funnel/Beaker people have gotten the wheel from Sumer or vice versa? It's doubtful. As the bird flies, it's about 1,200 miles from South Poland to Mesopotamia. Each culture probably invented the wheel independently.

Greatest Shortcuts

ERIE CANAL: CLINTON'S BIG DITCH

At the turn of the 19th century, the United States was bursting at its seams, and Americans were eyeing new areas of settlement west of the Appalachians. But westward overland routes were slow and the cost of moving goods along them was exorbitant.

The idea of opening the West by building a canal linking the Great Lakes with the eastern seaboard had been floated since the mid-1700s. It finally became more than wishful thinking in 1817, when construction of the Erie Canal began.

Citing its $7-million price tag, detractors labeled the canal "Clinton's Big Ditch" in reference to its biggest proponent, New York governor Dewitt Clinton. When completed in 1825, however, the Erie Canal was hailed as the "Eighth Wonder of the World." It cut 363 miles through thick forest and swamp to link Lake Erie at Buffalo with the Hudson River at Albany. Sadly though, more than 1,000 workers died during its construction, primarily from swamp-borne diseases.

The Erie Canal fulfilled its promise, becoming a favored pathway for the great migration westward, slashing transportation costs a whopping 95 percent, and bringing unprecedented prosperity to the towns along its route.

SUEZ CANAL: GRAND TRIUMPH

The centuries-old dream of a canal linking the Mediterranean and the Red Sea became reality in 1859 when French diplomat Ferdinand de Lesseps stuck the first shovel in the ground to commence building of the Suez Canal.

Over the next ten years, 2.4 million laborers would toil—and 125,000 would die—to move 97 million cubic yards of earth and build a 100-mile Sinai shortcut that made the 10,000-mile sea journey from Europe around Africa to India unnecessary.

De Lesseps convinced an old friend, Egypt's King Said, to grant him a concession to build and operate the canal for 99 years. French investors eagerly bankrolled three-quarters of the 200 million francs ($50 million) needed for the project. Said had to kick in the rest to keep the project afloat because others, particularly the British, rejected it as financial lunacy—seemingly justified when the canal's final cost rang in at double the original estimate.

The Suez dramatically expanded world trade by significantly reducing sailing time and cost. De Lesseps was proclaimed the world's greatest canal digger. The British, leery of France's new backdoor to their Indian empire, spent the next 20 years trying to wrest control of the Suez from their imperial rival.

PANAMA CANAL: SPECTACULAR FAILURE

When it came time to build the next great canal half a world away in Panama, everyone turned to de Lesseps to dig it.

But here de Lesseps was in over his head. Suez was a walk in the park compared to Panama. In the Suez, flat land at sea level had allowed de Lesseps to build a lockless channel. A canal in Panama, however, would have to slice through the multiple elevations of the Continental Divide.

Beginning in 1880, de Lesseps, ignoring all advice, began a nine-year effort to dig a sea-level canal through the mountains. This futile strategy, combined with financial mismanagement and the death of some 22,000 workers from disease and landslides, killed de Lessep's scheme. Panama had crushed the hero of Suez.

PANAMA CANAL: SUCCESS!

The idea of a Panama Canal, however, persevered. In 1903, the United States, under the expansionist, big-stick leadership of Theodore Roosevelt, bought out the French and assumed control of the project. Using raised-lock engineering and disease-control methods that included spraying oil on mosquito breeding grounds to eliminate malaria and yellow fever, the Americans completed the canal in 1914.

The Panama Canal, the last of the world's great canals, made sailing from New York to San Francisco a breeze. A trip that once covered 14,000 miles while circumnavigating the treacherous tip of South America was now a mere 6,000-mile pleasure cruise.

Worth the Paper It's Printed On: The History of Paper

Three cheers for Ts'ai Lun! Without him, there would be no daily gazette. Without him, there would be no dollar bills. Without him, there would be no fantastic historical diaries. Without him, no one could read this very book. Thanks to this gentleman from Lei-Yang, China, the world enjoys the gift of paper.

WHERE'S THE PAPER, BOY?

Ts'ai Lun's invention of paper dates to A.D. 105. However, paperlike papyrus had been produced in Egypt for more than 3,000 years prior. The word *paper* is even derived from *papyrus*. Ancient Egyptians developed it by hammering strips of the papyrus plant into a unified sheet for writing. They even sold it to the Greeks and Romans until around 300 B.C. With their papyrus supply cut off, Greeks and Romans turned to parchment, made from the skins of a variety of animals.

PAPER ON A ROLL

Ts'ai Lun was a member of the imperial court who became fascinated with the way wasps made their nests. Using that knowledge as a starting point, he took a mash of wood pulp and spread it across a coarse cloth screen. The dried fibers formed a sheet of pliable paper that could be peeled off and written on.

The new material quickly became a staple for official government business, for wrapping, and for envelopes. By the 7th century A.D., the Chinese had even invented toilet paper. A Chinese scholar at the time showed good judgment, observing, "Paper on which there are quotations or...the names of sages, I dare not use for toilet purposes."

PAPER GOES INTERNATIONAL

The art of papermaking remained in Asia for several centuries, spreading to Korea and Japan. Around A.D. 1000, papermaking reached the Middle East. Arabians used linen fibers in place of wood pulp, creating a higher quality paper. These superior products were in high demand, and exports increased. In this way, the art of papermaking reached Europe and flourished—particularly in Italy—by the 13th century.

The Italians took their papermaking very seriously, using machinery and standardized processes to turn out large amounts of top-notch paper. They used water power to run paper mills, created higher-quality drying screens, and improved the sizing process. A new coating was also developed to improve paper strength and reduce water absorbency.

(DON'T) STOP THE PRESSES!

When a German named Johannes Gutenberg developed the movable type printing press in the mid-1400s, the world of papermaking was changed forever. Books that were once hand-copied were now available in a mass-produced format. As the appetite for new books grew, so did the need for paper.

The New World was introduced to papermaking in the late 1600s, when the first paper mill was built in Mexico. A German immigrant named William Rittenhouse started the first paper plant in the British colonies in Philadelphia in 1690. In less than a century, 20 mills were producing paper in the colonies.

ALL THE NEWS(PAPER) THAT'S FIT TO PRINT

Much of the paper being produced in the mills was made from old rags, clothing, and other textiles, making a thick paper. Around 1840, a Canadian named Charles Fenerty used a fine wood pulp to create a thin, inexpensive paper known as "newsprint." However, he didn't pursue a patent for his work and his claim of invention was lost to others. Still, Fenerty's invention enabled newspapers to be printed more frequently.

IT'S IN THE BAG

Paper has proved to be a versatile material in uses that go far beyond writing and printing. Following the Civil

War, veteran Charles Stilwell returned to his home in Ohio and became a mechanical engineer. He noticed that paper bags used to carry groceries were not well made and wouldn't stand up on their own. He solved the problem, patenting a machine in 1883 that made paper grocery bags with a flat bottom and pleated sides. The style remains largely unchanged in the paper bags used today.

If Ts'ai Lun were still alive, he would most likely be amazed by how widespread his humble invention has become. In the modern world, it is virtually impossible to pass a day without picking up a book, a newspaper, an envelope, or a box. Readers, writers, and even shoppers owe him a debt of gratitude for making their world an easier place in which to live.

A Discovery of Biblical Proportions

While rounding up a stray animal near Qumran, Israel, in 1947, Bedouin shepherd Mohammed el-Hamed stumbled across several pottery jars containing scrolls written in Hebrew. It turned out to be the find of a lifetime.

News of the exciting discovery of ancient artifacts spurred archaeologists to scour the area of the original find for additional material. Over a period of nine years, the remains of approximately 900 documents were recovered from 11 caves near the ruins of Qumran, a plateau community on the northwest shore of the Dead Sea. The documents have come to be known as the Dead Sea Scrolls.

Tests indicate that all but one of the documents were created between the middle of the 2nd century B.C. and the 1st century A.D.

Nearly all were written in one of three Hebrew dialects. Most of the documents were written on animal hide.

The scrolls represent the earliest surviving copies of biblical documents. Approximately 30 percent of the material is from the Hebrew Bible. Every book of the Old Testament is represented with the exception of the Book of Esther and the Book of Nehemiah. Another 30 percent of the scrolls contain essays on subjects including blessings, war, community rule, and the membership requirements of a Jewish sect. About 25 percent of the material refers to Israelite religious texts not contained in the Hebrew Bible, while 15 percent of the data has yet to be identified.

Since their discovery, debate about the meaning of the scrolls has been intense. One widely held theory subscribes to the belief that the scrolls were created at the village of Qumran and then hidden by the inhabitants. According to this theory, a Jewish sect known as the Essenes wrote the scrolls. Those subscribing to this theory have concluded that the Essenes hid the scrolls in nearby caves during the Jewish Revolt in A.D. 66, shortly before they were massacred by Roman troops.

A second major theory, put forward by Norman Golb, Professor of Jewish History at the University of Chicago, speculates that the scrolls were originally housed in various Jerusalem-area libraries and were spirited out of the city when the Romans besieged the capital in A.D. 68–70. Golb believes that the treasures documented on the so-called Copper Scroll could only have been held in Jerusalem. Golb also alleges that the variety of conflicting ideas found in the scrolls indicates that the documents are facsimiles of literary texts.

The documents were catalogued according to which cave they were found in and have been categorized into biblical and non-biblical works. Of the eleven caves, numbers 1 and 11 yielded the most intact documents, while number 4 held the most material—an astounding 15,000 fragments representing 40 percent of the total material found. Multiple copies of the Hebrew Bible have been identified, including 19 copies of the Book of Isaiah, 30 copies of Psalms, and 25 copies of Deuteronomy. Also found were previously unknown psalms attributed to King David, and stories about Abraham and Noah.

Most of the fragments appeared in print between 1950 and 1965, with the exception of the material from Cave 4. Publication of the manuscripts was entrusted to an international group led by Father Roland de Vaux of the Dominican Order in Jerusalem.

Access to the material was governed by a "secrecy rule"—only members of the international team were allowed to see them. In late 1971, 17 documents were published, followed by the release of a complete set of images of all the Cave 4 material. The secrecy rule was eventually lifted, and copies of all documents were in print by 1995.

Many of the documents are now housed in the Shrine of the Book, a wing of the Israel Museum located in Western Jerusalem. The scrolls on display are rotated every three to six months.

Elevating Invention to New Heights

When Elisha Graves Otis and his sons began their elevator business in the 1850s, the solid brick buildings of America's cities had four-story height limits. By the 1920s, with the widespread adoption of safe, power-driven lifts, skyscrapers had replaced church steeples as the hallmarks of urban design.

Elevators to lift cargo have been around since the pyramidal ziggurats of ancient Iraq. In 236 B.C., the Greek scientist Archimedes used his knowledge of levers to deploy beast- and slave-drawn hoists. In 1743, technicians of French King Louis XV devised a "flying chair," with pulleys and weights running down the royal chimney, to carry his mistress, Madame de Pompadour, in and out of the palace's upper floor.

AN UPLIFTING BACKGROUND

A descendant of American Revolutionary James Otis, Elisha Otis won a hard-earned path to success. Born in Vermont in 1811, Otis was a stereotype of Yankee ingenuity. In the 1840s, as a senior mechanic in a bedstead factory in Albany, New York, he patented a railroad safety brake, critical to quickly and safely hauling freight in and out of the factories of the Industrial Revolution.

By 1852, Otis was a master mechanic at another bedstead firm in Yonkers, New York. He began tinkering with a safety lift for its warehouse, but the company went belly-up. Otis was mulling a move to California's Gold Rush country when a furniture maker asked him to build two safety elevators. A pair of workers at the manufacturer had died when a cable to their lift broke. Fighting off chronically poor health, Otis established his own company and set to work.

ALL SAFE

In 1854, Otis—looking quite distinguished in a full beard and top hat—took to a platform at the Crystal Palace exposition in New York. A rope had pulled his newfangled "hoisting apparatus" high up a shaft, its side open to public view. With a flourish, he waved an ax toward the nervous onlookers crowding the hall. Then, with a quick motion, Otis cleaved the rope with the ax. The onlookers gasped as the elevator began its downward plunge—only to suddenly stop after a three-inch fall. Elisha Otis tipped his hat and proclaimed: "All safe, gentlemen, all safe."

To ensure safety, Otis attached a wagon wheel's taut springs to the elevator ropes. "If the rope snapped," explained *Smithsonian* magazine, "the ends of the steel spring would flare out, forcing two large latches to lock into ratchets on either side of the platform."

Otis soon patented an elevator driven by a tiny steam engine, permitting small enterprises like retail stores to purchase their own lifts. Despite the technical wizardry, Elisha Otis's commercial success and business sense were limited. Two years after his successful demonstration—despite a follow-up exhibit at P. T. Barnum's Traveling World's Fair—sales of Otis elevators totaled less than $14,000 a year. Even if proceeds picked up, wrote Otis's son Charles, "Father will manage in such a way [as] to lose it all," going "crazy over some wild fancy for the future." Five years later, in 1861, Otis died at age 49 of "nervous depression and diphtheria." He left his two sons a business that was $3,200 in the red.

SUCCESS

Charles and Norton Otis proved better businessmen and rivaled their father as technicians, making important improvements to their useful device. By 1873, Otis Brothers & Company, revenues soaring, had installed 2,000 elevators into buildings. Replacing steam-powered lifts, their hydraulic elevators sat on steel tubes sunk into shafts deep below the buildings. An influx of water pushed the platforms up. Reducing the water pressure lowered the elevators.

Where hotel guests previously had preferred the accessible first floor, they now opted to "make the transit with ease" (as an Otis catalog boasted), to the top floors, which offered "an exemption from noise, dust and exhalations of every kind."

Though taken for granted today, elevators were the height of opulence then. One elevator from that era in Saratoga Springs, New York, was outfitted with chandeliers and paneled in ebony and tulipwood.

Riding the skyscraper boom, the Otis firm went from one noted project to another. In 1889, the firm completed lifts for the bottom section of the Eiffel Tower. Around 1900, it bought the patents to a related invention, the escalator. In 1913, the Otis firm installed 26 electric elevators for the world's then-tallest structure, New York's 60-story Woolworth Building. In 1931, Otis installed 73 elevators and more than 120 miles of cables in another record-breaker, the 1,250-foot Empire State Building.

SETTING THE CEILING

All the while, along with enhancements, such as push-button controls, came improvements in speed. Cities constantly changed their elevator "speed limits"—from a leisurely 40 feet a minute for Elisha Otis's original safety lifts, to a speedy 1,200 feet a minute in the 1930s, to today's contraptions, which, at 2,000 feet per minute can put a churning knot of G-force in the stomachs of passengers hurtling to their destination.

"That's probably as much vertical speed as most people can tolerate," says an Otis engineer.

Along the way, the elevator industry quashed early fears that speedy lifts were bad for people. In the 1890s, *Scientific American* wrote that the body parts of elevator passengers came to a halt at different rates, triggering mysterious ailments.

Like the earlier notion that fast trains would choke passengers by pushing oxygen away from their mouths, that theory has since been debunked.

The Opening of Tut's Tomb

There was a time when archaeology was commissioned privately by wealthy individuals. Some of these benefactors desired to advance historical knowledge, while others simply hoped to enhance their personal collections of antiquities. The much-heralded opening of the tomb of the Pharaoh Tutankhamun, better known today as "King Tut," represented one of the last hurrahs for these old days of archaeology.

WHO WAS KING TUT, ANYWAY?

King Tut was an ancient Egyptian ruler, or pharaoh. Tut ruled Egypt from 1333 B.C. to 1324 B.C., during what is referred to as the New Kingdom period. Sometimes called "The Boy King," he became pharaoh when he was 9 years old and died at age 19. Researchers believe Tut died after a leg injury became infected while his body was already fighting bone disease and malaria.

HOW WAS HIS TOMB LOCATED?

Finding the tomb required scholarship, persistence, patience, and lots of digging. A wealthy Englishman, Lord Carnarvon, sponsored one of the day's brightest archaeologists, Howard Carter. With Carnarvon's backing, Carter poked around in Egypt between 1917 and 1922 with little luck. Then, in November 1922, just as Lord Carnarvon was ready to give up, Carter uncovered steps leading down to a tomb marked with Tut's royal seals. Carter dashed off a communiqué to Carnarvon, telling him to get to Egypt, and fast.

WHAT HAPPENED NEXT?

Carnarvon wasted no time, and once the sponsor reached the scene, Carter was ready to cut his way into the tomb. Workers soon exposed a sealed doorway bearing Tut's name. Those present would witness the unveiling of history as Carter peered into the tomb. However, thanks to the meticulous nature of archaeology, work on Tut's tomb could only happen at a slow pace. The entire process stretched across the next decade.

WHAT WAS IN THERE?

The contents of the tomb were incredible. It was clear that ancient plunderers had twice raided the tomb for some smaller items. Although they did leave the place a mess, many amazing treasures remained. Carter and company catalogued piles of priceless artifacts, including gold statues and everything from sandals to chariots. Tut's mummified body had been placed in an ornate coffin, and canopic jars held his internal organs. In addition, two mummified premature babies, thought to be Tut's children, were found. Tut was also buried with everything he would need to be stylish in the afterlife, including ornate bows and gloves fit for a pharaoh. Scholars would spend years preserving and studying the artifacts in the tomb.

King Tut's tomb was the archaeological find of that decade—perhaps even the find of the 20th century.

Hope Floats

It was a given: Boats made of metal would sink straight to the bottom of the ocean. And a heavier-than-air flying craft? Impossibile!

Metal ships were so obviously an impossibility that no one made a serious effort to float steel until the end of the 18th century. Although an enterprising shipbuilder crafted a canal barge in 1787 and Robert Dickenson patented a design for an iron ship in 1815, it was generally accepted—with almost no discussion—that a seagoing vessel made of metal would sink.

Nine years passed between Dickenson's patent and the first attempt at building an iron passenger vessel (the Scottish vessel *Vulcan*), and no large navy dared field an iron-hulled fighting ship until Mexico bought one for its wars against Texas and Yucatán in the early 1840s.

At the other end of the transportation spectrum, the idea of a heavier-than-air flying machine was roundly ridiculed by the scientific establishment in the early 1900s. In 1902, the year before Wilbur and Orville Wright took their famous flight, the U.S. Navy's chief engineer declared the very idea "absurd." The following year, an eminent professor of mathematics and astronomy at Johns Hopkins University demonstrated to the world that a heavier-than-air craft was "scientifically impossible." Undeterred by this scientific pronouncement, the Wright brothers took their "flyer" to Kitty Hawk, North Carolina, and changed the world. Even after photographs circulated of the historic flight, the Wright brothers' hometown newspaper refused to print anything about their revolutionary contraption because, as the editor admitted, "We didn't believe it."

Groundbreaking Scientific Theories

As knowledge of the world becomes more complex, scientific breakthroughs become increasingly difficult to achieve. Here are a few examples of those whose work blazed a trail.

DISCOVERY OF CELL NUCLEI

Here's a quick scientific refresher: The fundamental unit of any living organism is the cell. Some organisms, such as bacteria and algae have only one cell. Others—people, for instance—have trillions of cells. Humans, plants, animals, bugs, and some single-celled organisms all have one thing in common, though: Each one of our cells has a nucleus. Robert Brown, a Scottish botanist, was the first to make this outstanding discovery.

Born in 1773, Brown studied medicine at the University of Edinburgh. Shortly after his graduation, he worked for five years as an army surgeon. Best known for traveling to distant lands and discovering hundreds of new plant species, Brown rose to prominence as a leading expert in botanic research. In 1831, while studying how herbs and orchids become fertilized, he noticed that each plant cell he studied had a structure in common. Brown decided to call this the *nucleus* of the cell, after the Latin word meaning "kernel," or "little nut."

Brown wasn't the first to see the nucleus of a cell. That credit went to the guy who perfected the microscope, Dutch scientist Antonie van Leeuwenhoek. Brown, however, was the first to recognize the nucleus's significance as the regulator of cellular activity. Brown's observations, research, and theories brought him much notoriety and fortune until his death in 1858.

GENETICS ACCORDING TO MENDEL

Do you know why a person might have her mom's red hair and not her dad's blonde hair? How about why someone has hazel eyes like Grandpa, even though Mom and Dad both have dark brown eyes? An Austrian-born geneticist named Johann Mendel, or Gregor Johann Mendel—the name by which he's more widely known—started to figure it out. Before Mendel, scientists didn't quite know how traits were passed from one generation to the next. There were several theories floating around, but most relied heavily on guesswork and didn't follow disciplined scientific methods to form their conclusions. Mendel changed that.

Mendel was born in 1822, the second of three children. He took an early interest in beekeeping and gardening, which guided his studies later in life. After joining a monastery and becoming a monk, Johann took the name Gregor and began studying the genetic variations of plants. He focused on the ordinary garden pea. After rigorous experimentation—on about 29,000 peas—and countless statistical and mathematical conclusions, Mendel discovered that peas pass their genetic traits to their offspring in a very specific way. How long would it take to count 29,000 peas, perform experiments, watch them grow, take notes on observations, and write a book about it? That's dedication!

Like most groundbreaking science throughout history, Mendel's theories weren't widely accepted when he published his work. His theories all but faded into history after his death in 1884. Some 20 years later, other scientists discovered Mendel's work and replicated his experiments. Suddenly, everyone flocked to Mendel's ideas. His discovery became known as "Mendel's Laws of Inheritance" and laid the foundation for modern genetics.

VITAMINS ACCORDING TO FUNK

What's the deal with food packaging listing all the important vitamins the food contains? Even something as sugary-good and delicious as breakfast cereal contains several "essential vitamins." What are these things? Let's turn the time machine back to 1911 and focus on a Polish biochemist by the name of Casimir Funk, the pioneer of vitamins.

The first part of the word *vitamin* comes from the Latin word for "life"; Funk knew that it would represent these life-giving, ammonia-based chemical compounds that he had discovered. These compounds can prevent diseases, help keep the body working in tip-top condition, and encourage healthy growth. Vitamins are essential for all multicelled life-forms to grow healthy and strong.

In Japan, it was discovered that a disease called beriberi, which attacks the nervous system, the heart, and the digestive system, was less likely to be contracted by those who ate lots of brown rice. No one knew why. Funk began experimenting by feeding rice to two groups of pigeons. He fed one group rice with its outer coating still on, and the other group rice with its coating removed. Funk discovered that the pigeons that ate the rice with the coating removed contracted beriberi, while the others remained healthy. After concentrating the nutrients he found in the coating of the rice, he labeled this concentration a *vitamine* in 1911.

Funk published a paper on his findings in 1912. His work was well received, especially by those suffering from beriberi and other diseases caused by vitamin deficiencies. He wasn't the only one to publish research on these nutrients at the time, but his was the most thorough and widely accepted.

THE DISCOVERY OF DNA STRUCTURE

Deoxyribonucleic acid—DNA for short—contains a living organism's genetic information. Although scientists have known about DNA since the 1860s, no one knew what it looked like. Imagine trying to find your way around a building without knowing anything about its appearance, inside or outside. You might know it's made of brick, concrete, steel, and glass, but what shape does it take? Where are the stairs and the elevator? James Watson and Francis Crick wanted to answer those very same questions about DNA—the building blocks of life.

Watson and Crick were molecular biologists from the United States and Great Britain, respectively. In the 1950s, they built their first model of DNA from metal and wire at Cambridge University in England. Watson and Crick gathered information from all over the place. They attended lectures, read scientific papers, looked at X-rays, and did their own experiments before deciding that building a model was the best way to approach the challenge. Unfortunately, their model failed. It failed so badly that the head of their department told them to cease all DNA research. But the pair couldn't let it go.

A breakthrough came in 1953 when a competing scientist, also frustrated in trying to discover the structure of DNA, shared his work (and his partner's, without her knowledge) with Watson and Crick. The new insight caused them to take a huge leap in thought. It had been widely accepted that DNA probably had two strands that wrapped around each other like a staircase. This is the double helix. Watson and Crick theorized that one side of the chain wound upward and the other side downward, with matching chemicals (base pairs) holding the two helices together. Discovering how the four base pair chemicals—adenine with thymine and cytosine with guanine—fit together was the final step in unlocking the mystery.

The structure of DNA is one of the most important discoveries of the last 100 years. It has influenced everything from food to medication to technology. In 1962, Watson, Crick, and Maurice Wilkins (the scientist who shared the work of his partner, Rosalind Franklin) won the Nobel Prize for Physiology/Medicine. Franklin did not receive the Nobel Prize, but only because the award is reserved for the living—she had died four years earlier.

The Story of Anesthesia

In the middle of the 19th century, three intoxicating solvents with bad reputations became the first crude "switches" that could turn consciousness off and on—paving the way for the revolution of painless surgical medicine.

On March 30, 1842, a doctor from rural Georgia laid an ether-soaked towel across the mouth and nose of a young patient with two cysts on his neck. The physician, Crawford Williamson Long, excised one of the growths while his patient was under. In the process, he made medical and scientific history. Long was perhaps the first doctor to use what is today called a "general anesthetic"—a substance that reduces or eliminates conscious awareness in a patient, allowing a doctor to perform incisions, sutures, and all other surgical procedures in between.

The "general"—which means complete or near-complete unconsciousness—is different from the targeted "local" anesthetic, an invention with origins shrouded in mystery. (Some ancient Inca trepanation rituals involved drilling a hole in the patient's skull to allow evil spirits to escape; to reduce the literally mind-numbing pain, the Incan shaman chewed leaves of the narcotic coca plant and spat the paste into the subject's wound.)

Unfortunately for Georgia's Dr. Long, the awards and acclaim that should have accompanied his medical milestone went to a dentist from Boston, who used ether four years later to knock out a patient in order to remove a tooth. Because this procedure was performed at the world-renowned Massachusetts General Hospital—and not at a backwoods country practice in the Deep South—the fame of the Massachusetts innovator, William T. G. Morton, was practically assured. Within two months of Morton's tooth extraction, doctors across Europe were toasting the Yankee who had invented pain-free surgery.

The story of the stolen spotlight, however, can't entirely be blamed on the prejudice of urban versus rural or North versus South. Long, who was known to enjoy the occasional "ether frolic," didn't publicize his use of ether as a general anesthetic until 1849, seven years after his initial use of it, and three years after Morton's world-acclaimed surgery.

WAKE UP, MR. GREEN. MR. GREEN?

By 1849, a London physician, John Snow, had invented a specialized ether inhaler to better administer a safe but effective dose of the painless surgical gas. Snow was responding to the need for more scientific care in the fledgling field of anesthesiology. Lethal doses of ether had already been administered in some botched surgeries, and Snow eventually championed chloroform, which, he would later write, is "almost impossible... [to cause] a death...in the hands of a medical man who is applying it with ordinary intelligence and attention."

Chloroform and ether each had their downsides, though.

Chloroform could damage the liver and occasionally even cause cardiac arrest. Ether required more time for the patient to both enter and exit the anesthetized state.

NOTHING TO LAUGH ABOUT

Some American practitioners championed a third popular early anesthetic: nitrous oxide or "laughing gas," although its reputation suffered when not enough of it was administered in an early demonstration during a tooth extraction at Harvard Medical School. When the patient cried out in pain, the dentist, Horace Wells, was booed out of the room. In a turn of tragic irony, Wells later became a chloroform addict and committed suicide in 1848, just three years after the Harvard fiasco.

By the 1860s and '70s, many surgeons had given up advocating one gas over another, preferring instead to use a mixture—either chloroform or nitrous oxide to induce anesthesia, followed by ether to keep the patient in an unconscious state.

Don't Touch That Dial! The Birth of Radio

At the turn of the 20th century, no one could have imagined today's world of shock-jocks, satellite radio, or streaming Internet audio. The idea of wireless communications was as foreign as the thought that humans would one day blast off into space.

IN THE BEGINNING

In the 1800s, discoveries by the German-born Heinrich Hertz and Scottish James Clerk Maxwell set the stage for Guglielmo Marconi's notable invention: the wireless telegraph. Because the Italian's home country offered no support for his work, Marconi sought and received aid from the British government. Soon the dots and dashes of Morse code were spanning the English Channel via radio signals. In 1897, Marconi founded the Wireless Telegraph & Signal Company Limited. A few years later, Morse code for the letter "S" was sent from the shores of England and received in Newfoundland, Canada. Marconi's radio signal had traveled across the Atlantic Ocean.

ENTER LEE DE FOREST

Inventor Lee De Forest took wireless communications a step further. The brilliant De Forest labored with many types of wireless telegraphs in the 1900s, building some for Western Electric and the U.S. Navy. In 1906, he invented the Audion, a three-element electron tube that amplified audio signals (the Audion was an improvement of the two-element device patented by Sir John Ambrose Fleming in 1904). The Audion was capable of transmitting Morse code and, more importantly, voice farther than ever before.

Initially, wireless transmissions were used strictly as communication for business or military operations. However, De Forest thought the new medium had greater potential. From 1907 to 1912, he invited members of the press to listen at receiving sets during several demonstrations in which he broadcast opera performances. These "broadcasts," were done using arc radio-telephones, which were less sophisticated

but more popular than the Audion at the time. Still, they showed that the wireless system could have much broader applications than its inventors had thought previously.

MOVING DOWN THE DIAL

By 1913, De Forest had sold his patent for the Audion to AT&T, which used the device to boost voice signals across the continent. In 1916, the Audion tube became an essential part of commercial transmitters.

De Forest's work was not limited to radio. In 1920, he developed the first sound-on-film process (Phonofilm) for the motion-picture industry. He received Hollywood's highest honor—an honorary Oscar—in 1959 for his "Pioneer Invention which brought sound to the Motion Picture." His process is still used today for analogue film audio.

The Underground Railroad

The very mention of the Underground Railroad reaches deep into the American psyche, invoking images of daring midnight escapes, secret tunnels, and concealed doors, as well as the exploits of thousands of daring men and women.

"...THAT ALL MEN ARE CREATED EQUAL"

The story of American slaves seeking escape from their masters long predates the invention of the railroad and its associated terms. The reasons for escape are easily understood and existed equally across slaves of all levels of privilege, from field hands to highly skilled laborers. Even before the Underground Railroad, escapees were often aided by individuals or organizations opposed to the institution of slavery. In fact, one prominent slave-holder—George Washington—complained in a letter that some of his fellow citizens were more concerned with helping one of his runaway slaves than in protecting his property rights as a slaveholder.

As the United States careened toward civil war, the arguments between supporters of slavery and those opposed to it became increasingly heated. Northern states began abolishing slavery on an individual basis—and became instant magnets for those fleeing servitude. In response, Congress passed Fugitive Slave Acts in 1793 and 1850, rendering escaped slaves fugitives for life, eligible for return to bondage on nothing more than the word of a white man. Any constable who refused to apprehend runaway slaves was fined. With the Northern states thus a less attractive final destination, runaways headed to Canada, where slavery had been outlawed in 1834. Meanwhile, abolitionist societies began to spring up, though a surprising number of them supported the return of escaped slaves to their masters, believing they could end the practice through moral persuasion rather than by violating the law.

ALL ABOARD

Despite hesitation on the part of some abolitionist societies, however, there were always individuals and groups who were sympathetic to the cause of the runaway slave and willing to place themselves at risk to help slaves find freedom. These benefactors ranged from white citizens to free blacks to other slaves willing to risk being beaten or sold for giving aid to runaways. Often, these protectors acted alone with little more than a vague idea of where to send a fugitive slave other than in the general direction of north. When a sympathetic individual discovered a runaway, he or she would often simply do what seemed best at the moment, whether that meant providing food and clothing, throwing pursuers off the track, or giving the slave a wagon ride to the next town.

By the 1840s, the expansion of the railroad was having a major impact on American society, and abolitionist activists quickly adopted its terminology. Conductors were those people who helped their passengers—runaway slaves—on to the next station or town, where they made contact with a stationmaster—the person in charge of the local organization. The most famous conductor, Harriet Tubman, was herself an escaped slave who risked no less than 19 trips back into slave country to guide out family members and others.

In some areas, small cells sprang up in which each person knew only about a contact on the next farm or in the next town, perhaps with the nebulous goal of somehow sending escapees into the care of well-known abolitionist societies in far-off Philadelphia or Boston. The image of one overriding national organization guiding the effort is largely a misleading one, but it was one encouraged by both abolitionists and slaveholders. The abolitionists were not hesitant to play up the romantic railroad imagery in an effort to bolster their fund-raising efforts. Their descriptions were so vivid that Frederick Douglass himself suggested they cease talking about it, lest they reveal their methods to their enemies. Likewise, Southern plantation owners were quick to play up the reports as proof that there was a vast abolitionist conspiracy bent on robbing them of their legal investment in slaves. As a result, some slave owners in border states converted their slaves to cash—selling them to the Deep South rather than risking their escape, a fate many slaves considered nothing less than a death sentence.

Efforts at undermining the institution of slavery did exist but were scarcely clandestine. Many abolitionists were quite open about their intentions.

"DEVILS AND GOOD PEOPLE, WALKING IN THE ROAD AT THE SAME TIME"

Despite the presence of Underground Railroad workers, the experience of a runaway slave was never anything other than harsh. On striking out for freedom, even successful escapees faced an ordeal that could last months. During their journey, they rarely had food, shelter, or appropriate clothing. Every white face was a potential enemy, as were some of their fellow black people, who were sometimes employed as decoys to help catch runaways. A false Underground Railroad even existed. Participants would take a runaway in and promise him safe passage only to deliver him to the local slave market. Often the escapees had no idea where they were going or the distance to be covered.

Although estimates vary wildly, one widely reported figure is that approximately 100,000 slaves found freedom either through their own initiative or with the aid of the Underground Railroad before the rest of those in bondage were freed during and after the Civil War. The history of the Railroad was largely written decades after the fact, and it is occasionally hard to separate reliable facts from the aged recollections of those justifiably proud of their efforts at securing liberty for their neighbors.

The Super Weapon That Fired Sound

One of the most important weapons of World War II never fired a shot and was helpless if attacked—but it brought down hundreds of enemy aircraft and saved thousands of lives.

The Radio Detection and Ranging device, or radar for short, was developed independently by researchers in eight nations, beginning nearly four decades before

World War II. The technology used sound waves to create an echo that would bounce off metal objects such as ships. When the echo returned to the sending unit, it could be analyzed to determine the distance—and to a lesser extent, the size—of the target.

RADAR DEVELOPMENTS

By the late 1930s, the major belligerents began crash programs to develop the technology for naval- and air-defense purposes. The U.S. Naval Research Laboratory, the British Meteorological Office, and the German *Kriegsmarine* had developed a series of workable sets by the time hostilities broke out in Europe.

As an island, Britain was protected by the sea and an impressive navy, but its vulnerability to air attacks meant it had much to gain from developing radar. In the late 1930s, it developed a rudimentary radar network called Chain Home. While the technology was merely adequate, the devices could be rushed into production in time to help defend the Home Isles against the *Luftwaffe* in the summer of 1940.

That same year, two British researchers at the University of Birmingham developed the cavity magnetron, a device that allowed radar operators to use higher-frequency sound waves that could be focused more tightly. Britain shipped the prototype in secrecy to the United States, where researchers at Massachusetts Institute of Technology (MIT) developed production models for an improved radar system.

The Soviet Union had one ship-based radar device, the Redut-K system, in place by 1940. For its radar needs, the U.S.S.R. relied heavily upon sets from the United States and Britain.

Neither Germany nor Japan elected to keep pace with the Allies' radar development. Although Germany's Freya system was more sophisticated than the early Chain Home units fielded by Great Britain, Germany had only eight operational units in the field at the outbreak of the war. Further, Freya technology did not accurately determine altitude.

The *Kriegsmarine* received several Freya systems in 1937, and in 1942, after the conquest of France and the Low Countries, the Third Reich established the Kammhuber Line, a chain of radar installations running from Denmark to central France. These stations helped the Germans defend against Royal Air Force attacks, but by 1942 British air planners could overwhelm the flak and air interception potential of the Kammhuber Line by concentrating bomber formations.

Japanese radar lagged well behind advances in the United States and Europe. Early in the war, the Japanese also created a small number of reasonably effective naval-radar sets. They relied on some captured devices, including a British model taken after the fall of Singapore and two American devices found when the army overran the Philippines.

RADAR EVOLVES

Ships were equipped with radar to spot enemy craft (and periscopes) at night. De Havilland Mosquito fighter-bombers and Bristol Beaufighter fighters, among others, were fitted with miniature radar sets: These allowed the fighters to locate *Luftwaffe* bombers at night or in bad weather.

As radar became more sophisticated, air forces began using countermeasures, such as chaff (metal strips that reflected radar waves). On radar devices, chaff looked the same as a formation of enemy planes. Raiders would drop the metal strips to divert interceptor resources from their planned targets and protect their planes.

Story of Braille

How do you make up your own language? Louis Braille did it with equal parts perseverance and creativity.

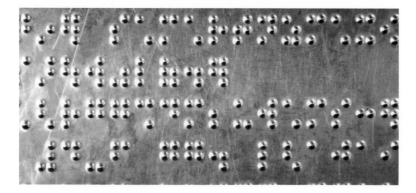

INGREDIENTS

Take Louis Braille, an inquisitive, creative boy who lost his sight as the result of an accident he suffered at age three. Send him on scholarship to the National Institute for Blind Youth in Paris. Expose him to a cumbersome and slow method of reading. Now add a soldier from the French army by the name of Charles Barbier and his system, sonography, which used raised dots to represent sound. Barbier developed this language to help soldiers communicate in the field without drawing attention to their positions, but the army eventually nixed it for being too complex.

THE MIXTURE

These ingredients laid the basis for Braille's work. Over time, Braille developed a system that could be recognized and understood by passing one's fingers over characters made up of an arrangement of one to six embossed points. Braille is a system made up of rectangles; each rectangle, or cell, has two columns and three rows. Each position has a particular number assigned to it—in the left column, moving down, the positions are numbered one, two, and three; in the right column, moving down, the positions are four, five, and six. Raised points at particular positions have particular meanings. For example, points raised at positions one, three, and four represent the letter *m*.

Because this system can be written with a stylus and a slate, the visually impaired have a means by which they can both read and write. Not only is that a recipe for further learning and efficient communication, but it's also a method by which they can increase their independence.

CHAPTER 2
MOMENTOUS EVENTS

"God Wills It!"

Pope Urban II's call to arms in 1095 set off a war for the Holy Land that would change the course of history for the next thousand years.

The First Crusade (1096–1099) was born of a pope's desire to safeguard the holy sites of Palestine for Christian pilgrims and to assert papal influence over the kingdoms of Western Europe. One sermon, given in late 1095, did more to change the course of the second millennium than any other speech in history.

BIRTH OF THE CRUSADES

The Crusades were born of a desire to roll back an Islamic empire that stretched from Afghanistan to northern Spain. In the 7th and 8th centuries, while many European nobles spent their time fighting one another, a wave of Arab-led, Islam-inspired armies thundered across North Africa, Central Asia, the southern Mediterranean, and the Iberian Peninsula, gobbling up huge chunks of territory—many of which were torn out of the predominantly Orthodox Christian Byzantine Empire.

It did not take a political genius to figure out that Western Europe could set aside brewing political and social differences by uniting against a dangerous enemy espousing a different religion. In 1074, Pope Gregory VII issued a call for Christian soldiers to rush to the aid of the Byzantine Empire; they may have been Orthodox Christians, but they were Christians nonetheless, and they were being threatened by the great imperial powers of the age, the Islamic Caliphates.

The publicity surrounding the pope's pleas attracted the attention of Christian pilgrims, who began visiting the Holy Land in record numbers. When priests began spreading tales of Muslims robbing Christian pilgrims on their way to Jerusalem, Europe was ripe for a battle over Palestine.

URBAN'S CALL TO ARMS

Enter Pope Urban II. Elected in 1088, this savvy French priest carried out his diplomatic duties with finesse. When Emperor Alexius I of Byzantine called for help against the Muslim hordes, Urban was happy to oblige. He summoned bishops from all over Europe to Clermont, France. Once some 300 bishops had assembled in an open-air forum, Urban gave them a barn-burner of a sermon. He exhorted the Christians of Europe to take up arms, to drive back the Muslim armies occupying the Holy Land.

Knowing his real audience was the kings, princes, and nobles who would be asked to send soldiers into battle, the cagy Urban was quick to point out the material benefits of a conquest of eastern lands. He proclaimed:

"This land which you inhabit, shut in on all sides by the seas and surrounded by the mountain peaks, is too narrow for your large population; nor does it abound in wealth; and it furnishes scarcely food enough for its cultivators...Enter upon the road to the Holy Sepulcher; wrest that land from the wicked race, and subject it to yourselves."

The kicker, of course, was that the crusaders would have a spiritual carte blanche to kill and conquer, all with divine sanction. "God has conferred upon you above all nations great glory in arms. Accordingly undertake this journey for the remission of your sins, with the assurance of the imperishable glory of the kingdom of heaven," Pope Urban II said.

Urban's sermon wowed the bishops and nobles in attendance, who left the council chanting, *"Deus vult!"* ("God wills it!"). European peasants, knights, and nobles answered Urban's call, and over the next year, a hodgepodge of crusaders (generally grouped into the unsuccessful "People's Crusade" and the more successful "Princes' Crusade") took up the Cross, looking for heavenly rewards, material treasure, and great victory.

CONQUEST OF THE HOLY LAND

The Crusades didn't get off to much of a start. The thousands of hungry, ill-supplied peasants who had joined the People's Crusade were neither trained nor organized, and they were quickly massacred once they set foot into Seljuk Turk territory. But the roughly 7,000 knights of the Princes' Crusade managed to capture Antioch, north of Jerusalem, in 1098. The following year, the crusading army—about 1,500 knights, supported by some 12,000 men-at-arms—reached Jerusalem, which it captured after a brief siege. The crusaders capped their victory by massacring men, women, and children of all faiths in all sections of the holy city. They set up the Kingdom of Jerusalem, which they ran as a Christian fiefdom until it fell to Saladin and his Arabian armies in 1187.

ECHOES THROUGH THE AGES

The First Crusade set in motion a seesaw battle between the Christian west and the Islamic east that lasted another two centuries. As chunks of the Holy Land fell to one army or another, Urban's successor popes used the Crusades as a way to unite Europe. But the Crusades, and the orgies of blood they incited, left a bitter legacy. The rancor that the Crusades caused among both Christians and Muslims has persisted to this day, and even now the word "crusader" evokes very different feelings among Westerners and Middle Easterners.

A Short History of History's Shortest War

NO FRIEND OF THE QUEEN

On the morning of August 27, 1896, the new Sultan of Zanzibar, Khalid bin Barghash, a 29-year-old who had been sultan for a mere 48 hours, awoke to the sight of five British warships anchored in the harbor just outside his palace.

Things were not going well for young Khalid. Although he enjoyed the support of his people and had a legitimate claim to the throne, the British were unhappy with him. In a clearly worded communication to Queen Victoria, Khalid had expressed his hope that friendly relations could continue between his country and England but stated he could not abandon the "house of his fathers." Meanwhile, the British felt they could not tolerate the rule of a man they considered far too traditional.

AN UNEVEN CONTEST

To convince Khalid that he should abdicate the throne, the British hastily assembled a fleet that, though small in number, boasted the largest concentration of artillery ever deployed in East Africa at the time. The Zanzibari navy consisted of a showpiece called the *Glasgow*, a wooden steam vessel equipped with ancient, muzzle-loading cannons. Nevertheless, the crew of the *Glasgow* affirmed their allegiance to Khalid—as did almost 3,000 Zanzibari soldiers and loyalists who occupied the palace—and prepared for a siege.

They didn't have to wait long. Just before the deadline hour of 9:00 A.M., the captain of the *Glasgow* was rowed to his ship, which was anchored amongst the formidable British vessels. The British took this as a sign that Khalid would not capitulate without a lesson.

A SHORT LESSON

At exactly 9:05 A.M., the British warships opened fire. The *Glasgow* bravely returned fire but was soon sinking in the harbor's shallow water. The barrage on the palace was intense. By some estimates, more than a thousand shells were fired by the British ships that morning. Finally, the smoke obscuring the target and the complete cessation of return fire caused the British to stop their bombardment. The royal harem next to the palace was fiercely ablaze, and the palace itself had been reduced to ruins. The war was over—less than 40 minutes after it had begun.

AFTERMATH

Khalid survived the bombardment and fled to the German embassy where he was given sanctuary for several weeks before escaping to Dar es Salaam. The royal palace was utterly destroyed and never rebuilt. The harem, however, was soon replaced. Khalid's British-supported successor, Hamoud bin Mohammed, made good on his promise to begin the modernization of his country—his first step was to outlaw slavery; for this he was decorated by Queen Victoria.

A Violent Run for the Roses

Power—not flowers—was at stake in the Wars of the Roses, a series of battles and skirmishes between two branches of England's royal family. The Lancaster clan had the throne, and the York clan wanted it. Then the tables turned and turned again.

These civil wars were called the Wars of the Roses because the symbol of the House of Lancaster was a red rose while the symbol of the House of York was a white rose.

A FAMILY FEUD

One drawback of monarchies is that they often lead to quarrels over whose turn it is to sit on the throne. Brother turns against brother, son against father, and so on. More than 500 years ago, such a disagreement between noble cousins grew into a squabble that split England's ruling class into armed camps and repeatedly tore up the countryside.

The House of Lancaster and the House of York were branches of the royal Plantagenet family, descendants of King Edward III, who ruled from 1327 to 1377. The Wars of the Roses began in 1399, when Henry of Bolingbroke, a grandson of Edward III, ended the disastrous reign of his cousin, Richard II, and took the throne himself. Also known as the Duke of Lancaster, the new king, now Henry IV, founded the Lancastrian Dynasty. He passed his scepter down to son Henry V, who in turn passed it to his then nine-month-old son, Henry VI in 1422.

THE YORKIST CLAIM

Lancastrian heirs might have continued this streak indefinitely, but pious Henry VI preferred the spiritual realm of prayer to his worldly kingdom, which sorely needed leadership. Worse, the king developed a mental disorder resulting in periodic breakdowns.

After Henry VI's 1453 breakdown, the powerful Earl of Warwick appointed the Duke of York to fill in as protector of the realm. York, an able leader, was also a descendent of Edward III and boasted a family tree that arguably made him a better claimant to the crown than the sitting king.

York earned the fierce enmity of the queen, Margaret of Anjou, who wielded more actual power than her husband did and who feared York would steal the throne. Battles ensued, beginning in 1455, with York defeating the royal forces more than once. In 1460, Lancastrian forces killed York in a sneak attack. The Yorkist cause passed to his 18-year-old son, Edward, who won a decisive battle, ran King Henry and Queen Margaret out of the country, and had himself crowned Edward IV in 1461.

The wars went on, however, as the new king clashed with his father's old supporter, the Earl of Warwick. For a time, Warwick got the upper hand and put addled King Henry back on the throne. Edward prevailed in 1471, however, and maintained order until his death in 1483.

THE FIGHT RESUMES AND ENDS

Edward IV's young son briefly succeeded him as Edward V, but the boy's uncle, brother of the late king, appears to have pulled a fast one. The uncle pushed little Eddie aside and became Richard III, one of England's most notorious monarchs. His notoriety is based on the widespread belief that Richard III murdered his two defenseless young nephews—Edward V and a younger brother.

For that reason and others, Richard lost the backing of many nobles, who flocked to support another royal claimant, Henry Tudor, the Earl of Richmond. A Welshman, this new contender also descended from Edward III on the Lancaster side.

Tudor famously killed Richard III in battle and became Henry VII, founder of England's Tudor Dynasty. He married the Yorkist heiress, the late Edward IV's daughter Elizabeth, in 1485, consolidating the family claim and ending, finally, the Wars of the Roses.

Francisco Pizarro and the Ransom of an Emperor

In 1532, Spanish explorer Francisco Pizarro—already a veteran of several expeditions to the New World—set out to conquer Peru. Through a combination of good luck and sheer hubris, Pizarro and his men met with astounding success. The most notable victim of their conquest was the Incan Emperor Atahualpa, who sought to bargain for his freedom by playing on Spanish greed.

FORTUNE FAVORS THE BOLD

The morning of November 16, 1532, found Francisco Pizarro in a dodgy position. The would-be conqueror of Peru and his 150 men were camped in the village of Cajamarca to await the arrival of Atahualpa, emperor of the Inca. Atahualpa had agreed to come and meet the strangers, and he was bringing his army with him. The approach of the Inca—80,000 strong—could be seen for miles. The disparity in numbers caused no small amount of worry among the Spanish soldiers.

Pizarro, however, was made of sterner stuff. Hernán (Hernando) Cortés had conquered the Mexican Aztecs scarcely a dozen years earlier against similar odds, and Pizarro was determined to do no less. Regardless of the risks, Pizarro would go through with the meeting, promising to receive Atahualpa as a "friend and brother." If the emperor proved too strong, the ruse would be kept up; if not, the audacious plan was to demand political submission. And if Atahualpa refused, he would be taken hostage.

THE CONQUISTADOR VS. THE LIVING GOD

The emperor entered town as the sun was setting, leaving most of his army to camp half a mile away. However, he was still personally accompanied by a retinue that numbered in the thousands. Atahualpa himself, bedecked in emeralds and wearing a crown and parrot feathers, rode ensconced on a gold-plated litter carried high by 80 finely dressed Incan nobles. When he momentarily halted, he was greeted by Vincente de Valverde, a Dominican friar accompanying the Spanish expedition. Valverde invited Atahualpa to dine with Pizarro—possibly a trick designed to separate the emperor from his men. When the invitation was declined, Valverde extended a crucifix and Bible, asking the Incan ruler to embrace the Christian faith and acknowledge himself a vassal of the Holy Roman Emperor. Predictably enough, Atahualpa did not look favorably on the friar's suggestion and slapped the book into the dirt. Atahualpa then demanded that the Spanish return all that they had stolen since arriving in his lands.

Tempers flared, and the Spanish opened fire. Concealed cannons tore into the massed Incan party, and Spanish horsemen cut through the crowd like a scythe. The sudden eruption of fire and noise, combined with the strange sight of mounted troops, threw the native force into a panic. After just minutes, the Incas were unable to mount an effective defense. They trampled each other underfoot, and many suffocated from the mass of their own numbers. The emperor's bearers continued to physically support him as long as they lived, some trying to carry him on their shoulders after their hands were severed by Spanish swords. But escape proved impossible, however, and the emperor was captured. Pizarro himself saved Atahualpa's life by parrying a blow from a Spanish soldier intent on killing the Incan leader. The clash was nothing less than a slaughter. Incan estimates put the number of local troops killed at 10,000 in less than two hours.

BUSINESS AS USUAL

After the bloody encounter, Atahualpa quickly adopted a pragmatic outlook. As he dined that night with Pizarro from seats overlooking a courtyard still littered with fallen men, Atahualpa dismissed the episode as "the fortune of war." The emperor blamed himself for the outcome; he had underestimated the Spaniards. Aware of the European thirst for treasure, Atahualpa sought to buy his freedom, promising to fill a room measuring 22 feet by 17 feet by 8 feet high with gold in exchange for his release. Pizarro agreed, and a cooperative Atahualpa continued to manage his empire from captivity. His top priority was to instruct his people to collect the ransom.

Pizarro was certainly interested in Atahualpa's gold, but he was in no particular hurry to see the process of collection finished. Atahualpa's word was the equivalent of divine law to the Incan people—a very useful resource for an outnumbered invader trying to control an entire country. However, as the treasure accumulated and

Spanish reinforcements arrived, Atahualpa became progressively less important to the Spanish. The situation climaxed in August 1533, when Atahualpa was led forth to be executed by burning at the stake—a sentence that was generously reduced to death by garrote when the emperor requested baptism into the Christian faith at the last moment. After asking Pizarro to care for his children, Atahualpa was strangled to death as the assembled Spaniards offered prayers for his soul.

THE SOLDIER GETS A TONGUE-LASHING

The massacre of the Incas was largely seen as inconsequential at the time—a mere product of the way war was conducted. Indeed, the Incan leader himself said had their positions been reversed, he would have sacrificed some of the Spanish to the sun god while castrating the rest and using them to guard his concubines. However, many in Spain saw the execution of Atahualpa, a captive under Spanish protection, as murder and a scandal. Perhaps most notably, Holy Roman Emperor Charles V regarded the execution of a monarch by a common soldier as a bad precedent. Charles officially reprimanded Pizarro—another blow to the prestige of the fortune-hunting soldier.

European guilt notwithstanding, there is no record of the millions of pesos Pizarro sent back to Spain being anything but welcome.

Plight of the Pilgrims: Journey to the New World

When the Pilgrims began their voyage to the New World, they didn't expect to sail on the *Mayflower*, nor did they plan to land at Plymouth Rock.

DESTINATION: HOLLAND

The story of the Pilgrims begins back in 1606—14 years before they set sail on the *Mayflower*. A band of worshippers from Scrooby Manor, who belonged to the Church of England, decided that they would rather worship God according to the Bible than indulge in the extra prayers and hymns imposed by the church. However, separating from the church was easier said than done. In England, it was illegal to be a Separatist. Risking imprisonment, the worshippers escaped to Holland, a land of religious tolerance. But their time in Holland was a mixed blessing. Although they worshipped freely, they feared their children were becoming more Dutch than English.

DESTINATION: HUDSON RIVER

Meanwhile, English noblemen were seeking brave, industrious people to sail to America and establish colonies in Virginia (which extended far beyond the Virginia we know today). They offered the Separatists a contract for land at the mouth of the Hudson River, near present-day New York City.

Led by William Brewster and William Bradford, the Separatists accepted the offer and began preparing for their voyage. They even bought their own boat: the *Speedwell*. In July 1620, they sailed to England to meet 52 more passengers who rode in their own ship, the *Mayflower*. The Separatists, who called themselves "Saints," referred to these new people as "Strangers."

DESTINATION: UNKNOWN

The *Speedwell* should have been called the *Leakwell*. After two disastrous starts, the Saints abandoned hope of her sailing again. On September 6, they joined the Strangers on the *Mayflower.*

The *Mayflower* was just 30 yards long—about the length of three school buses. The 50 Saints rode in the "tween" deck, an area between the two decks that was actually the gun deck. Its ceilings were only about five feet high.

Accommodations in the rest of the boat were hardly better. Cramped into close quarters were 52 Strangers, 30 crewmen (who laughed at the seasick landlubbers), 2 dogs (a spaniel and a mastiff), barley, oats, shovels, hammers, tools, beer, cheese, cooking pots, and chamber pots. There may have been pigs on board, too.

As they journeyed across the Atlantic, storms and rough waters pushed them off course. After 65 days on the high seas, they realized they were nowhere near the Hudson River. Instead, they sighted the finger of Cape Cod—more than 220 miles away from their destination.

Though they were far from the land contracted for the English colony, the settlers saw their arrival in the New World as an opportunity to build a better life. In November 1620, more than 40 free men (Saints and Strangers alike) signed the Mayflower Compact. They agreed to work together for the good of the colony and to elect leaders to create a "civil body politic."

BUT WHAT ABOUT PLYMOUTH ROCK?

After anchoring in a harbor (which is now Provincetown), the Saints formed three expeditions to locate a suitable place to live. One expedition ventured 30 miles west to a place called "Plimouth," which had been mapped several years earlier by explorer John Smith.

The settlers first noticed a giant rock, probably weighing 200 tons, near the shore. The land nearby had already been cleared. Likely, more than a thousand native people had lived there before being wiped out by an epidemic.

Some remaining bones were still visible.

In December 1620, the group decided to make Plymouth its settlement. According to legend, each passenger stepped on Plymouth Rock upon landing. If this actually happened, leader William Bradford did not record it.

By springtime, half of the *Mayflower's* passengers would be dead. Yet their accomplishments remain important. Helped by native people, the Saints and Strangers would live and work together to form one of the first British settlements in North America.

Henry VIII Is Excommunicated

On April 20, 1534, a taut rope on the Tyburn gallows in Westminster, England, strangled the life out of a popular and charismatic 28-year-old nun. Elizabeth Barton, the "Holy Maid of Kent"—a veritable homegrown Joan of Arc—had become an unlikely public spokesperson against King Henry VIII. She claimed that God had told her in a series of visions that he would visit his vengeance upon the middle-aged king for defiling a divinely consecrated marriage. The king responded as he would to others who stood in his way (such as Sir Thomas More, author of *Utopia*, the following year): Their opposition made them traitors, and therefore they had to die.

The previous year, Henry had, in defiance of the pope, divorced his first wife Catherine of Aragon to marry one of Catherine's ladies-in-waiting, the charming and sophisticated (and pregnant!) Anne Boleyn. To marry Anne, Henry had not only to contravene the reigning Catholic Church's prohibition against divorce, he also had to face actual excommunication. The Church of England was the phoenix that ultimately rose from the ashes.

Although some accounts of Henry VIII's break with Rome portray the split as "King Marries Temptress, Starts Own Church," the historical reality is slightly more complex.

On one hand, Henry was undeniably enraptured with Anne. Seventeen of his love letters to her—nine of them in French, a language in which both were fluent but precious few other Englishmen were—can be perused today at the Vatican Library in Rome. Henry tells his mistress in one missive that "for more than a year, [I've been] struck with the dart of love." Elsewhere he implores her to give "body and heart to me, who will be, and has been, your most loyal servant."

On the other hand, Henry's extramarital love life wasn't happening in a historical vacuum either. In 1529, what historians now call "the Reformation Parliament" clapped economic and political shackles upon the operation of the Catholic Church in England—regulating excessive fees the church had levied for burials, reducing clergy's ability to make money on the side, and eliminating their de facto above-the-law status by subjecting church officials to the same secular courts as any English commoner.

THE CHURCH OF ENGLAND IS BORN

What momentum Parliament had established was compounded by the rise of two reformist members of Henry's court in the early 1530s: Thomas Cranmer (made Archbishop of Canterbury, the highest ecclesiastical position in the nation, in 1533) and Thomas Cromwell (Henry VIII's chief advisor and principal minister). The two Thomases provided the political and theological muscle to establish an independent church body and, with it, put the squeeze on the Catholic Church in England. In 1533, Cranmer ensured swift approval by his bishops of the annulment of King Henry's first marriage, while at the same time Cromwell's Act in Restraint of Appeals effectively set forth the English monarch as ruler of the British Empire, rendering the papacy irrelevant by deriving a monarch's authority directly from God. The pope, thanks to Cromwell's legislative strong-arm, suddenly had no claim over true English subjects.

Naturally, Pope Clement VII did not take this news lightly. After three months of threats, Clement excommunicated Henry VIII from the Catholic Church in September 1533. Though true theological reform of the fledgling Anglican Church into a bona fide Protestant sect would have to wait for the brief but outsized reign of Henry's only son, Edward VI (reign 1547–53), there was no turning back. The Church of England had been born.

THE FALLOUT

Both the inspiration and the instigators of the break with Rome eventually met with gruesome deaths: Boleyn lasted all of three years as her king's wife before Henry, in concert with Cromwell, rounded up four courtiers and servants to Boleyn who were all variously charged with luring Boleyn away from the marriage bed. Boleyn was swiftly tried for adultery and beheaded in May 1536. Cromwell lasted only four more years before he too became victim to the capricious whims of his monarch. For proposing a disastrous fourth marriage to Anne of Cleves, Cromwell faced a rigged jury, was found guilty of treason and, at the king's behest, faced the further brutality of an inexperienced executioner. Three unsuccessful ax blows drew out Cromwell's pain before a fourth severed his head, which was then boiled and placed on a pike on London Bridge.

Cranmer outlived his king and his king's son, only to face the furies of the brutally anti-Protestant queen "Bloody" Mary Tudor (reign 1553–58).

Yet perhaps it was Anne Boleyn herself who bequeathed the greatest legacy in the form of her daughter, who took the reins of power at Queen Mary's death. The frail young princess, not expected to survive any longer than her siblings, instead enjoyed a prosperous 45 years on the throne as perhaps England's greatest monarch, Queen Elizabeth I. Under Elizabeth, the Church of England established itself as the ecclesiastical force that underpinned the rise of a true global empire—on whose influence, to this day, the sun never sets.

America's First Foreign War

Ever wonder why the U.S. Marines will fight their country's battles "to the shores of Tripoli"? Here's the answer.

William Eaton, acting as an agent for the U.S. government, disembarked from the brig USS *Argus* at Rosetta, Egypt, on November 26, 1804. His mission was to find Hamet Karamanli, the former ruler of Tripoli and leader of the Barbary pirates. A few years earlier, Hamet had been deposed in a coup and was replaced by his brother Yusuf Karamanli. Eaton wanted Hamet to become the ostensible leader of an expedition to overthrow Yusuf, whose pirates had captured the frigate USS *Philadelphia* and its crew.

UNSAFE AT SEA

For hundreds of years Britain, France, and Spain had been paying the Barbary pirates to leave their ships alone. The United States, now independent from Britain and no longer under its system of payments, became fair game. Captured sailors of all nations wound up in the dungeons of Tripoli, Tunis, and Algiers. In 1785, after the merchant ships *Maria* and *Dauphin* were captured, the significance of the problem was brought home to all Americans.

Secretary of State Thomas Jefferson thought the United States had but three choices: Pay tribute to the pirates like the European countries; forbid American vessels to sail in the Mediterranean; or go to war. Representative Robert Goodloe Harper made a stirring promise to spend "millions for defense, but not one cent for tribute."

Congress authorized $688,888.82 for the construction of six frigates, but an agreement on tribute was reached none-theless. America would pay the pirates yearly tribute and a ransom of more than a million dollars. America had a merchant fleet to protect, and this arrangement was cheaper than full-scale war.

THIS MEANS WAR

By 1797, John Adams had become president, and all of the American captives had either died in prison or been released. For four years there was relative peace. Then, near the end of Adams's term, Yusuf Karamanli decided that the Americans weren't paying enough and declared war on the United States. That was fine with most Americans, who were fed up with paying tribute.

Jefferson became president in 1801, and he saw America's fight with the Barbary pirates as a test of the young nation's mettle. He sent a six-ship squadron to the Mediterranean under Commodore Edward Preble.

Those six ships had to patrol more than 1,200 miles of coastline—a nearly impossible task. This was made more difficult when the frigate *Philadelphia* ran aground off Tripoli and was captured in October 1803. Something had to be done—such a warship could not be left in the hands of pirates.

On the night of February 16, 1804, Lieutenant Stephen Decatur led a raiding party into Tripoli harbor. He and his crew annihilated the Tripolitan prize crew and burned the *Philadelphia*—a feat Britain's Admiral Nelson called "the most daring act of the age."

The crew of the *Philadelphia* and Americans from other ships were still in the dungeons of Tripoli, however. The American captives couldn't just wait out the war. Those with exploitable talents were treated well, but most were tortured and forced to do hard labor. Men were dying, committing suicide, or converting to Islam and fighting for Yusuf.

RESCUE PARTY

Back in Egypt, Eaton managed to scrape together 90 of Hamet's followers, joined by 50 Greek mercenaries, 20 Italian gunners, and a fire-eating Englishman named Farquhar. About 300 Bedouin Arab cavalry completed the local contingent.

Eaton wanted to include 100 U.S. Marines from the fleet, but Captain Samuel Barron refused. In the end, the only Americans who took part were Eaton, Lieutenant Presley O'Bannon of the marines with a sergeant and a few enlisted soldiers, and Midshipman Pascal Paoli Peck, U.S. Navy.

On March 5, 1805, the expedition set off across the desert. Lacking most necessary equipment, they stumbled into Bomba on April 15. They had been 25 days without meat and 15 days without bread; for two days, they'd eaten nothing at all. Smoke signals brought the USS *Argus*, which had ample provisions and one of two promised cannons.

THE BATTLE OF DERNA

The group set off for Derna, arriving on April 26. When an attempt to negotiate with the governor of the town brought the response "your head or mine," Eaton attacked.

After his force took significant casualties and had its one cannon put out of action, Eaton decided on an all-out assault. Brandishing a sword and leading his force, Eaton swept through the barricades and took the town. Resistance collapsed, and the governor took refuge within his harem. It wasn't Tripoli, but it was close enough. Yusuf agreed to release American captives and leave American ships alone. The war was over.

A Bodyguard of Lies: The Allied D-Day Deception

Germany had more than enough muscle behind the guns and forts of the Atlantic Wall to blast any seaborne invasion to rags—but only if that muscle were all brought to bear swiftly in the right place. The main ingredient of this Allied mission, therefore, had to be trickery.

"In wartime, truth is so precious that she should always be attended by a bodyguard of lies."
—Winston Churchill

The Germans expected the Allies to attempt to invade France, but they weren't sure when or how. They knew that the Allies would likely invade as near as possible to British ports to avoid aero-naval interception and remain in range of air cover. Royal Air Force fighters had enough range to cover Normandy and the Pas de Calais region just opposite Dover. As the Allies saw it, Calais was the quickest sail, but also the Atlantic Wall's sharpest teeth. Instead, they planned to endure the longer ride to Normandy, where the defenses were less formidable.

Of course, any invasion could fail if the Germans guessed its location in advance. To throw them off, the Allies contrived Operation Bodyguard, a key part of which was Operation Fortitude, a deception plan divided into North and South. Fortitude North's goal was to tie German troops up in Norway with a phantom invasion. Fortitude South would try to mislead the Germans about the real invasion's location while disguising the fact that the Allies were planning multiple landings.

Fortitude North faked radio traffic to make the small northern UK garrison sound like a full army preparing to invade Norway. Thanks to achievements in broadcasting and recording, a single radio truck could simulate the chatter of a divisional headquarters; a signals battalion could simulate an army.

Fortitude South's first job was to convince the Germans that the blow would land near Calais, with possible feints elsewhere. After the troops landed in Normandy, the second phase of Fortitude South would be to maintain the impression that a second, heavier blow was still to come at the Pas de Calais. The planners invented a fictitious army under General Patton: the 1st U.S. Army Group (FUSAG), complete with nonexistent infantry divisions.

Germany depended upon its spies to confirm or contradict what the Allies were really planning. But its intelligence turned out to be unreliable—every German spy reporting from Britain was actually working for the British.

PREPARED FOR ANY EVENTUALITY

General Dwight D. Eisenhower assumed that if at any point the Germans figured out the plans for the true D-Day invasion, Field Marshal Erwin Rommel would hurl every tank toward the Normandy beaches while the invasion was at sea—perhaps disobeying even Hitler—to prepare a lethal reception. Eisenhower took the possibility seriously enough to prepare two speeches before the invasion: one praising its success and one taking all blame if it failed.

As it was, D-Day achieved tactical surprise. The Germans had indeed expected the Allies to storm the Pas de Calais sector. Noting that "known" FUSAG elements had not yet been sent into battle, they committed only a portion of the panzer reserve to holding off the Allied forces at Normandy. The rest were withheld to oppose FUSAG's expected second invasion. This gave the Allies those few crucial days needed to reinforce and consolidate the

Normandy beachhead. The second invasion came not in June at the Pas de Calais, but on August 15, 1944, in southern France.

FUSAG never fired one rifle shot, yet it helped defeat Germany. The Allies' D-Day deception effort went down as one of the best-executed ruses in military history.

The Plot to Assassinate President Truman

Puerto Ricans have sought independence from the United States for decades. In 1950, two ardent nationalists took matters into their own hands. Their target? President Harry Truman.

The Puerto Rican Nationalist Party was spoiling for a fight. They had tried to reach independence through electoral participation, but by the 1930s, leader Dr. Pedro Albuzu Campos began advocating a campaign of violent revolution.

In 1936, Albuzu Campos was charged with conspiring to overthrow the government and was incarcerated. He spent the next six years in jail in New York. When he finally returned to Puerto Rico in 1947, the tinder of *nacionalismo puertorriqueño* was bone-dry and smoldering.

THE MATCH IS LIT

On October 30, 1950, Nationalists seized the town of Jayuya. With air support, the Puerto Rico National Guard crushed the rebellion. Griselio Torresola and Oscar Collazo, two *nacionalistas*, decided to retaliate at the highest level: the president of the United States.

They had help from natural wastage. The White House, which looks majestic from the outside, has been quite the wretched dump at many points in its history. By

1948, it was physically unsound, so the Truman family moved to Blair House while the White House was being renovated. It would be a lot easier to whack a president at Blair House than it would have been at the White House.

THE ATTEMPT

At 2:20 P.M. on November 1, 1950, Torresola approached the Pennsylvania Avenue entrance from the west with a 9mm Luger pistol. Collazo came from the east carrying the Luger's cheaper successor, the Walther P38. White House police guarded the entrance. Truman was upstairs taking a nap.

Collazo approached the Blair House steps, facing the turned back of Officer Donald Birdzell, and fired, shattering Birdzell's knee. Nearby Officers Floyd Boring and Joseph Davidson fired at Collazo through a wrought-iron fence without immediate effect. Birdzell dragged himself after Collazo, firing his pistol. Bullets from Boring and Davidson grazed Collazo in the scalp and chest—seemingly minor wounds. Collazo sat down to reload.

Officer Leslie Coffelt staffed a guard booth at the west corner as Torresola took him unaware. Coffelt fell with a chest full of holes. Next, Torresola fired on Officer Joseph Downs, who had just stopped to chat with Coffelt. Downs took bullets to the hip, back, and neck. He staggered to the basement door and locked it, hoping to deny the assassins entry. Torresola advanced on Birdzell from behind as the officer engaged Collazo and fired, hitting his other knee. Birdzell lost consciousness as Torresola reloaded.

AN OUNCE OF LUCK

Weapon recharged, Oscar Collazo stood, then collapsed from his wounds. At that moment, a startled Truman came to the window. Torresola was 31 feet away. If he had looked up at precisely the right moment, the Puerto Rican nationalist would have achieved his mission.

Despite three chest wounds, Officer Coffelt forced himself to his feet, took careful aim, and fatally shot Griselio Torresola. Coffelt staggered back to the guard shack and crumpled.

Collazo survived and was sentenced to death. President Truman commuted Collazo's sentence to life imprisonment in 1952, shortly before leaving office.

Officers Downs and Birdzell recovered. Officer Leslie Coffelt died four hours later. The Secret Service's day room at Blair House is now named the Leslie W. Coffelt Memorial Room.

CHAPTER 3

LOWLIGHTS

The Ancient Pedigree of Biological and Chemical Warfare

Considered the pinnacle of military know-how, biological and chemical warfare has actually been around for millennia.

CHINA'S DEADLY FOG

Inventors of gunpowder and rockets, the Chinese were also among the first to use biological and chemical agents. Fumigation to purge homes of vermin in the 7th century B.C. likely inspired the employment of poisonous smoke during war. Ancient Chinese military writings contain hundreds of recipes for such things as "soul-hunting fog," containing arsenic, and "five-league fog," which was laced with wolf dung. When a besieging army burrowed under a city's walls, defenders struck back. They burned piles of mustard in ovens, then operated bellows to blow the noxious gas at the subterranean attackers. In the 2nd century A.D., authorities dispersed hordes of rebellious peasants with a kind of tear gas made from chopped bits of lime.

ANCIENT GREEK POISONS

The ancient Greeks were also experienced with biological and chemical weapons. Herodotus wrote in the 5th century B.C. about the Scythian archers, who were barbarian warriors dwelling near Greek colonies along the Black Sea. By his account, Scythian bowmen could accurately fire an arrow 500 yards every three seconds. Their arrows were dipped in a mixture of dung, human blood, and the venom of adders. These ingredients were mixed and buried in jars until they reached the desired state of putrefaction. These poison arrows paralyzed the lungs, inducing asphyxiation.

A bioweapon figured prominently in the First Sacred War. Around 590 B.C., fighters from the city of Kirrha attacked travelers on their way to the Oracle of Delphi and seized Delphic territories. Enraged at the sacrilege, several Greek city-states formed the League of Delphi and laid siege to Kirrha. For a time, the town's stout defenses stymied the attackers. However, according to the ancient writer Thessalos, a horse stepped through a piece of a buried pipe that brought water into the city. A medicine man named Nebros convinced the Greeks to ply the water with the plant hellebore, a strong purgative. The defenders, devastated by diarrhea, were rendered too weak to fight, and the Greeks captured the town.

FLYING CORPSES SPREAD THE BLACK PLAGUE

In 1340, during the siege of a French town during the Hundred Years' War, it was reported that catapults "... cast in deed horses, and beestes stynking...the ayre was hote as in the myddes of somer: the stynke and ayre was so abominable." Vlad the Impaler, the 15th-century Romanian warlord and real-life model for Dracula, used a similar method against Turkish foes.

Scholars believe that this ghastly biological warfare tactic played a big role in spreading the worst plague in human history: the bubonic plague, better known as the Black Death. In 1346, merchants from Genoa set up a trading outpost in Crimea, which was attacked by Tartars, a warlike horde of Muslim Turks. However, during the siege, the attacking forces were decimated by the plague. To even the score, the Tartars catapulted the corpses of plague victims over the walls of the Genoan fortress.

Horrified, the Genoan merchants set sail for home. In October 1347, their galleys, carrying rats and fleas infested with the Black Death, pulled into Genoa's harbor. Within several years, the plague would spread from Italy to the rest of Europe, felling more than a third of its population.

A POX ON ALL THEIR HOUSES

In America, biological warfare darkened the French and Indian War. In 1763, during the vast rebellion of Native Americans under Chief Pontiac, the Delaware tribe allied with the French and attacked the British at Fort Pitt. Following the deaths of 400 soldiers and 2,000 settlers, the fort's defenders turned to desperate means.

William Trent, the commander of Fort Pitt's militia, knew that a smallpox epidemic had been ravaging the area, and he concocted a plan. He then made a sinister "peace offering" to the attackers. Trent wrote in his journal, "We gave them two Blankets and an Handkerchief out of the Small Pox Hospital. I hope it will have the desired effect." It did. Afflicted with the disease, the Delaware died in droves, and the fort held.

Trent's idea caught on. Soon after the Fort Pitt incident, Lord Jeffrey Amherst, the British military commander in North America, wrote to Colonel Henry Bouquet, "Could it not be contrived to send the Small Pox among those disaffected tribes of Indians? We must on this occasion use every stratagem in our power to reduce them." Amherst, for whom Amherst, Massachusetts, is named, added, "Try every other method that can serve to Extirpate this Execrable Race."

THE DA VINCI FORMULA

Even Leonardo da Vinci—one of history's best and brightest minds—dabbled with chemical weapons. The artist, and sometime inventor of war machines, proposed to "throw poison in the form of powder upon galleys." He stated, "Chalk, fine sulfide of arsenic, and powdered verdigris [toxic copper acetate] may be thrown among enemy ships by means of small mangonels [single-arm catapults], and all those who, as they breathe, inhale the powder into their lungs will become asphyxiated." Ever ahead of his time, the inveterate inventor even sketched out a diagram for a simple gas mask.

African Exploration

The meeting of Dr. David Livingstone and Henry Morton Stanley in 1871 was a high point in African exploration that would leave as its legacy one of the most brutal colonial empires in history.

It had been five years since Scottish missionary David Livingstone disappeared into central Africa to find the source of the Nile; young war correspondent Henry Morton Stanley saw potential for a great story, and he convinced newspaper magnate James Gordon Bennett Jr. to finance his search.

DR. LIVINGSTONE, I PRESUME?

Stanley led a party of guards and porters into uncharted territory in March 1871. Within a few days, his stallion was dead from tsetse flies, and dozens of his carriers had deserted with valuable supplies. Over the months that followed, his party was decimated by tropical disease and endured encounters with suspicious Africans.

Finally, on November 10, 1871, Stanley found the ailing Livingstone at a settlement on Lake Tanganyika in present-day Tanzania. Legend has it Stanley greeted the missionary with the words, "Dr. Livingstone, I presume?" Stanley's dispatches to the *New York Herald* were the media sensation of the age.

FAME AND MISFORTUNE

Upon his return to Great Britain, Stanley was met with public ridicule, as many scientists and journalists questioned the veracity of his accounts. Though his book, *How I Found Livingstone*, was a best seller, Stanley was deeply wounded by his detractors.

Indeed, Stanley was an unlikely hero. Born John Rowland, he was the illegitimate child of a disinterested mother. He left Britain at age 17 to work as a deckhand on a merchant vessel. He jumped ship in New Orleans and took the name of an English planter, who he claimed had adopted him; historians doubt that Stanley ever met the man.

Stanley's life was an improbable series of adventures. He served, unremarkably, on both sides during the Civil War and worked unsuccessfully at a variety of trades before trying his hand at journalism. He reported on the Indian wars in the West and on the Colorado gold rush. Before he embarked upon his search for Livingstone, Stanley accompanied a British military expedition into Abyssinia and became known for his colorful dispatches.

THE GREATEST AFRICAN EXPLORER

Stanley may have found in Livingstone the father figure he never had. His accounts of the missionary created a portrait of a saintly doctor who, inspired by his opposition to Africa's brutal slave trade, had opened the continent to Western civilization and Christianity.

Livingstone died in 1873, and Stanley served as a pallbearer at his funeral. A year later, Stanley set out on another epic expedition to complete Livingstone's work. Over the next three years, Stanley established Lake Victoria as the source of the Nile and led his party down the uncharted Congo River—a 2,900-mile course that traversed the continent.

Though acclaimed as the greatest African explorer, Stanley's accounts of his methods—such as whipping African porters and gunning down tribespeople—brought public outrage in Britain. After examining his original notes and letters, however, some historians believe that he often exaggerated his exploits to elevate his legend.

A JOURNEY FOR LEOPOLD

Unable to persuade the British government to employ him, Stanley undertook a third journey in 1879 under the sponsorship of Belgium's King Leopold II. He established trading posts along the Congo River, laying the foundation for a vast colonial empire that would exploit the rubber, copper, and ivory trades at the expense of millions of African lives.

This third expedition led to the scramble for Africa among European nations, culminating in the Berlin Conference of 1885, which divided the continent among colonial powers. Leopold II established his rights to the so-called Congo Free State, his private enterprise encompassing most of the Congo Basin. Historians estimate that millions of Congolese were murdered or died from disease or overwork under Leopold's regime, inspiring Joseph Conrad's novel *Heart of Darkness*.

A final African expedition between 1887 and 1889 further tarnished Stanley's name. Sent to rescue a dubious ally in southern Sudan, he left behind a rear column whose leaders—former British army officers and aristocrats—degenerated into sadism.

Finally marrying and adopting a son, Stanley retired from exploration to write books and conduct lecture tours. He won a seat in Parliament in 1895 and was knighted by Queen Victoria in 1899. He died in 1904 at the age of 63. Although he was considered a national hero, he was denied burial next to Livingstone at Westminster Abbey due to his mixed reputation.

The Great Hunger

When the Irish potato crop failed in 1845, it caused a tragedy that devastated the nation for generations.

The Ireland of 1845 was a British colony where many of the people labored as tenant farmers for English landlords, raising grain and grazing cattle for export. To feed themselves, the Irish cultivated potatoes on tiny plots of land. Some historians assert that by the 1840s, half of Ireland's population of eight million ate nothing but potatoes. Then an unwelcome visitor—a mold called *Phytophthora infestans*—arrived from America. This "potato blight" rotted the precious tubers in the fields. Between 1845 and 1849—a period that became known, in Gaelic, as *An Gorta Mór*, "The Great Hunger"—an estimated one million Irish died of outright starvation or from the diseases that stalked in famine's wake. Another 1–1.5 million left their homeland in desperation. Some went to England or to British colonies such as Australia. Many others chose to cut their ties to the British Empire and cross the Atlantic to settle in the United States— where they played a crucial role in building America. Seventy years after the famine ended, Ireland's population was only about half of what it had been in 1845.

The British government organized some relief efforts, but the effort was a classic case of too little, too late. Worse was the fact that even at the height of the famine, the Emerald Isle still teemed with food—for export to England! The fiercely independent, mostly Catholic Irish had long resented British domination of their island, but the timid British response to the famine fueled a new spirit of rebellion that culminated in Ireland's full independence in 1937.

Tragedy at the Haymarket

What began as a campaign for an eight-hour workday ended with a bloody event that sent ripples far and wide.

It was the mid-1880s, and Chicago was in a state of transition. Industry was growing more and more mechanized—good news for the corporations that were able to increase profits and lower wages, but bad news for workers who were putting in 12 to 14 grueling hours a day, 6 miserable days a week. In October 1884, the Federation of Organized Trade and Labor Unions set a goal to make the eight-hour workday standard, even if nationwide strikes were necessary to make that goal a reality. The stage was set.

THE CALM BEFORE THE STORM

On May 1, 1886, hundreds of thousands of workers across the country took to the streets in support of an eight-hour workday. The first few days of the strike were relatively peaceful, but all hell broke loose on May 3, when police killed several unarmed strikers near Chicago's McCormick Reaper Works.

Workers gathered in a light rain in Haymarket Square on the West Side on May 4. Mayor Carter Harrison Sr. stopped by in a show of support for the workers, then left early when it appeared that all was peaceful. The rest, as they say, is history—and a somewhat murky history at that, as many questions remain about what unfolded in the incident now known as the Haymarket Riot.

Once the mayor left, the police inspector sent in the riot police to disperse the crowd. Soon after, a bomb went off. The police opened fire. A few short minutes later, eight policemen were dead, and scores of workers and bystanders had been injured.

THE FALLOUT

Police immediately swept across the city in search of the bomber. They arrested eight known anarchists (August Spies, Samuel Fielden, Oscar Neebe, Michael Schwab, Louis Lingg, George Engel, Adolph Fischer, and Albert Parsons) and charged them with the crime. After a well-publicized trial, the jury (which included a Marshall Field's sales rep and not a single industrial worker) returned guilty verdicts for all eight, even though only two of the men were even at the Haymarket the night of the incident. The men had clearly been tried for their incendiary speeches leading up to the Haymarket incident, not for anything they had actually done. Seven of the men were sentenced to death, and the show trial resulted in protests around the world.

SERIOUSLY, WHO THREW THE BOMB?

Spies, Fischer, Engel, and Parsons were hanged on November 11, 1887; Lingg had committed suicide in prison one day earlier. Governor Altgeld pardoned Schwab, Fielden, and Neebe in 1893. To the present day, no one is sure who threw the bomb, but most historians believe it was one of two anarchists who were present at the protest that day: Rudolph Schnaubelt or George Meng—neither of whom was ever arrested for the crime.

Historians consider Haymarket one of the seminal events in the history of labor, and its legacy resonates to this day. The Haymarket defendants stand as icons of the American labor movement and are remembered with rallies, parades, and speeches around the world on the anniversary of the bombing.

Most important, however, is the spirit of assembly that can be traced back to Haymarket. Today, monuments stand at the corner of Des Plaines and Randolph streets (near the spot where the bomb was thrown) and in Forest Park, Illinois, at the grave of Spies, Fischer, Engel, Parsons, and Lingg. These symbols are poignant reminders of a critical time in labor history.

Ghosts of a Murdered Dynasty

The fate of Russia's imperial family remained shrouded in mystery for nearly a century.

THE END OF A DYNASTY

In the wake of Russia's 1917 uprisings, Tsar Nicholas II abdicated his shaky throne. He was succeeded by a provisional government, which included Nicholas and his family—his wife, Tsarina Alexandra; his four daughters, Grand Duchesses Olga, Tatiana, Maria, and Anastasia; and his 13-year-old son, Tsarevich Alexei—under house arrest.

When the radical Bolshevik party took power in October 1917, its soldiers seized the royal family and eventually moved them to the Ural Mountain town of Yekaterinburg, where they were held prisoner in the House of Special Purpose. As civil war waged between the "White" and "Red" factions in Russia, the Bolsheviks worried that the White Army might try to free the royal family and use its members as a rallying point. When White troops neared Yekaterinburg in July 1918, the local executive committee decided to kill Nicholas II and his family.

The bedraggled imperial family was rudely awakened by their captors in the middle of the night. The sounds of battle echoed not far from the home that had become their makeshift prison, and the prisoners were ordered to take shelter in the basement. Tsar Nicholas had to carry Alexei, who was gravely ill.

After a long wait, the head jailer reappeared, brandishing a pistol and backed by ten men armed with rifles and pistols. He declared, "Because your relatives in Europe carry on their war against Soviet Russia, the Executive Committee of the Ural has decided to execute you." Raising his revolver, he fired into Tsar Nicholas II's chest as his family watched in horror.

With that shot, the militia opened fire. Bullets ricocheted around the room as family members dove for cover.

None made it. Those who clung to life after the firing stopped were dragged into the open and set upon with rifle butts and bayonets until the moaning stopped.

A BUNGLED DISPOSAL OF BODIES

The bodies were taken into the Siberian forest, stripped, and thrown into an abandoned mine pit. The corpses were visible above the pit's shallow waterline. Fearing that the bodies would be discovered, the communist officials tried to burn them the following day. When that did not work, they decided to move the bodies to a deeper mine pit farther down the road. The truck got stuck in deep mud on the way to the mines, so the men dug a shallow grave in the mud, buried the bodies, and covered them with acid, lime, and wooden planks, where they remained untouched until their discovery in 1979.

In his official report, the lead executioner Yakov Yurovsky stated that two of the bodies were buried and burned separately, giving rise to speculation that one or two of the Romanov children escaped the massacre. Several pretenders came forth claiming to be Tsarevich Alexei, heir to the Russian throne, and his sister Grand Duchess Maria. But the most famous of the "undead Romanovs" was young Anastasia.

DID ANASTASIA SURVIVE?

Anastasia, the fourth daughter of Nicholas and Alexandra, was 17 at the time of the executions. At least ten women have stepped forward claiming to be the lost grand duchess. The most famous of these was Anna Tchaikovsky.

Two years after the murders, Ms. Tchaikovsky—who was hospitalized in Berlin after an attempted suicide—claimed to be Anastasia. She explained that she had been wounded but survived the slaughter with the help of a compassionate Red Army soldier, who smuggled her out of Russia through Romania.

Anna bore a striking physical resemblance to the missing Anastasia, enough to convince several surviving relatives that she was indeed the last of the imperial family. She also revealed details that would be hard for an impostor to know—for instance, she knew of a secret meeting between Anastasia's uncle, the grand duke of Hesse, and Nicholas II in 1916.

Other relatives, however, rejected Anna's claim, noting, among other things, that Ms. Tchaikovsky refused to speak Russian (although she understood the language and would respond to Russian questions in other languages). A drawn-out German court case ended in 1970 with no firm conclusions.

Anna, later named Anna Anderson, died in 1984. It was not until DNA evidence became available in the 1990s that her claim to imperial lineage could finally be disproved.

THE ROMANOV GHOSTS

But what of the hidden remains?

After the location of the royal resting place was made public in 1979, nine skeletons were exhumed from the muddy pit. The bodies of the royal couple and three of their children—Olga, Tatiana, and Anastasia—were identified by DNA tests as Romanov family members. Their remains, as well as those of four servants who died with them, were interred in 1998 near Nicholas's imperial predecessors in St. Petersburg.

By all accounts, 11 people met their deaths that terrible night in July 1918. In late August 2007, two more sets of remains were found in a separate grave near Yekaterinburg. Based on results of DNA analysis that was completed in 2009, experts agree that the sets of remains were those of Tsarevich Alexei and Maria.

Who Betrayed Anne Frank?

Anne Frank and her family thwarted Nazis for two years, hiding in Amsterdam until someone blew their cover.

Annelies Marie Frank was born in Frankfurt am Main, Germany, on June 12, 1929. Perhaps the most well-known victim of the Holocaust, she was one of approximately 1.5 million Jewish children killed by the Nazis. Her diary chronicling her experience in Amsterdam was discovered in the Franks' secret hiding place by friends of the family and first published in 1947. Translated into more than 60 languages, *Anne Frank: The Diary of a Young Girl* has sold more than 30 million copies and is one of the most widely read books in the world.

The diary was given to Anne on her 13th birthday, just weeks before she went into hiding. Her father, Otto Frank, moved his family and four friends into a secret annex of rooms above his office at 263 Prinsengracht on July 6, 1942. They relied on friends and trustworthy business associates, who risked their own lives to help them. Anne poignantly wrote her thoughts, yearnings, and descriptions of life in the secret annex in her diary, revealing a vibrant, intelligent young woman struggling to retain her ideals in the direst of circumstances.

On August 4, 1944, four or five Dutch Nazi collaborators under the command of an Austrian Nazi police investigator entered the building and arrested the Franks and their friends. The family was deported to Auschwitz, where they were separated and sent to different camps. Anne and her sister, Margot, were sent to Bergen-Belsen, where they both died of typhus in 1945, a few weeks before liberation. Anne was 15 years old. Otto Frank was the only member of the group to survive the war.

Dutch police, Nazi hunters, and historians have attempted to identify who betrayed the Franks. Searching for clues, the Netherlands Institute for War Documentation (NIWD) has examined records on Dutch collaboration with the Nazis, the letters of Otto Frank, and police transcripts dating from the 1940s. The arresting Nazi officer was also questioned after the war by Nazi hunter Simon Wiesenthal, but he could not identify who informed on the Franks. For decades suspicion centered on Willem Van Maaren, who worked in the warehouse attached to the Franks' hiding place, but two police investigations found no evidence against him.

British author Carol Anne Lee believes it was Anton Ahlers, a business associate of Otto's who was a petty thief and a member of the Dutch Nazi movement. Lee argues that Ahlers informed the Nazis to collect the bounty paid to Dutch civilians who exposed Jews. She suggests he may have split the reward with Maarten Kuiper, a friend of Ahlers who was one of the Dutch Nazi collaborators who raided the secret annex. Ahlers was jailed for collaboration with the Nazis after the war, and members of his own family, including his son, have said they believe he was guilty of informing on the Franks.

Austrian writer Melissa Müller believes that a cleaning lady, Lena Hartog, who also worked in the warehouse, reported the Franks because she feared that if they were discovered, her husband, an employee of Otto Frank, would be deported for aiding Jews.

The NIWD has studied the arguments of both writers and examined the evidence supporting their theories. Noting that all the principals involved in the case are no longer living, it concluded that neither theory could be proved.

In 2016, the Anne Frank House museum published its own research suggesting that the Franks may have been uncovered by chance instead of being betrayed. Nazi officers investigating illegal work and/or ration fraud at the warehouse may have accidentally stumbled upon the Franks hiding in the annex.

Baseball's Darkest Hour

Baseball's Golden Age was preceded by its darkest hour: the 1919 World Series-fixing scandal.

The young lad who emerged from the crowd outside a Chicago courthouse on that September day in 1920 was described by the *Chicago Herald-Examiner* as "a little urchin." He was said to have grabbed Shoeless Joe Jackson by the coat sleeve. The newspaper's report of the exchange went like this:

"It ain't true, is it?" the lad said.

"Yes, kid, I'm afraid it is," Jackson replied.

"Well, I'd never have thought it," the boy exclaimed.

Nowhere did the newspaper report that the boy demanded, "Say it ain't so, Joe," although this version of the story was passed down through the generations. A few years before his 1951 death, Jackson told *Sport Magazine* that the story was made up.

What *is* so is this: Members of the 1919 Chicago White Sox committed baseball's cardinal sin, deliberately losing the World Series to the Cincinnati Reds for pay.

The White Sox took the American League pennant, and the Sox were favored to defeat Cincinnati in the World Series—heavily favored, in some gambling circles. By all accounts, Sox infielder Chick Gandil made contact with known gamblers. He immediately involved 29-game-winner Eddie Cicotte, and others followed: Jackson, pitcher Claude Williams, infielders Buck Weaver and Swede Risberg, outfielder Oscar "Happy" Felsch, and utility man Fred McMullin. Some of the players would play lead parts in the fixing of games. Others—notably Weaver and some say Jackson—had knowledge of the plan but were not active participants.

When the Series began, the players were promised $100,000 to throw the games. By the time the Reds won the Series in eight games, the payout was considerably less, and whispers about what had taken place began swelling to a roar. Sportswriters speculated about a possible fix even before Cincinnati wrapped up the Series, but nobody wanted to believe it could be true.

CONSPIRACY TO DEFRAUD THE PUBLIC

The 1920 season began with rumors about gambling in other big-league dugouts. In September a grand jury convened to examine instances of gambling in the game, and the jury soon looked at the 1919 World Series. Eight White Sox players were called to testify, and several admitted knowledge of the fix. All eight were indicted for conspiracy to defraud the public and injure "the business of Charles Comiskey and the American League." Although the group was acquitted due to lack of evidence, the damage had been done.

Judge Kenesaw Mountain Landis, baseball's newly appointed commissioner, suspended all eight players for life. It was a crushing blow for Chicago, and for Weaver and Jackson in particular. While Gandil had received $35,000 and Cicotte $10,000 for the fix, Weaver received nothing. Actually, it was proven that he had turned down an invitation to participate in the scam. And Jackson, considered one of the greatest outfielders and hitters in the history of the game, hit .375 with six RBI in the 1919 Series while playing errorless defense.

Many still clamor for Shoeless Joe to be enshrined in the Hall of Fame, arguing that his numbers support his claim that he did nothing to contribute to the fixing of the 1919 World Series. However, the $5,000 he accepted from the gamblers sealed his fate as a tragic figure in baseball's most infamous 20th-century scandal.

Say it ain't so, Joe.

Too bad it is.

The Kent State Tragedy

Few know the full story of the tragic shootings at Kent State, which was obscured by inaccurate media reports and protracted legal proceedings against the National Guardsmen involved.

During a demonstration at Kent State University on May 4, 1970, members of the Ohio National Guard shot and killed four students and wounded nine others. To fully understand the reasons behind the tragedy, it is crucial to know the historical context.

Kent State was one of several universities organizing and protesting against President Richard Nixon's expansion of the Vietnam War. Nixon had been elected in 1968, partly on the promise that he would end the war.

In early 1969, the president took a few steps to decrease U.S. involvement in Southeast Asia, but on April 30, 1970, he approved a massive military operation in Cambodia. Antiwar protests were planned on many college campuses, which angered Nixon, who referred to protesters as "bums."

STATE OF EMERGENCY

On May 1, an antiwar rally was held on the Commons of Kent State University, with plans for another rally on May 4. Many young people created a disturbance in downtown Kent that night, committing acts of vandalism and frightening citizens. Business owners blamed Kent State students, but witnesses observed that outsiders—including a motorcycle gang and other nonstudents—were among those making trouble.

Police used tear gas to disperse the crowd, and Mayor Leroy Stanton declared a state of emergency. This allowed Governor James Rhodes to approve a request for the National Guard.

On May 2, the ROTC building went up in flames. Although the arsonists were never identified, the press and townspeople blamed the protesters. Demonstrators openly confronted police and slashed the hoses of the firefighters who came to extinguish the flames.

Guardsmen were stationed all over campus on May 3, and everything remained relatively quiet until Governor Rhodes held a press conference. He warned that he would use force to stop the demonstrators, comparing them to fascists, vigilantes, and communists. New clashes between the protesters and law enforcement broke the calm with more rocks and tear gas.

THE RIGHT TO DISSENT

On May 4, the university attempted to ban the rally, but by noon a crowd of 1,500 people had gathered. Students believed they had a right to hold a rally, and the presence of the guardsmen fostered resentment.

About 100 young, inexperienced National Guardsmen in riot gear stood on the edge of the Commons. When General Robert Canterbury ordered the demonstrators to disperse, police and guardsmen drove across the Commons to push the crowd out of the way.

One particular group of National Guardsmen—their bayonets fixed—followed some students to the top of Blanket Hill, where those students dispersed. Then about a dozen guardsmen turned around and shot down the hill in the direction of the other demonstrators and students. Some fired in the air and at the ground, while others shot directly into the crowd.

More than 60 shots were fired, killing four students and wounding nine others. Those killed were Allison Krause, Jeffrey Miller, Sandra Scheuer, and William Schroeder. Two of the dead were not even part of the protest: Sandra Scheuer was merely walking to class, and Schroeder—an ROTC student—was simply a bystander. The guardsmen retreated to the Commons, where angry students confronted them. A handful of faculty members and student leaders defused the situation.

The school was closed, and students were ordered to leave campus. These shootings galvanized 4.3 million participants to protest the war on 500 college campuses around the country. State and federal investigations were launched, with criminal and civil charges brought against some of the guardsmen. In 1970, President Nixon's own Commission on Campus Unrest concluded that the "indiscriminate firing of rifles into a crowd of students and the deaths that followed were unnecessary, unwarranted, and inexcusable." However, none of the guards were convicted or punished, partly due to interference from Governor Rhodes.

AFTERMATH

Character assassinations of the dead and wounded students followed, which were spread to the press and circulated among top officials in Washington, with FBI Director J. Edgar Hoover calling one of the victims "nothing more than a whore." The jury in a 1975 civil trial ruled that none of the guardsmen were legally responsible for the deaths and injuries, but the judge ordered a new trial when it was discovered that one of the jurors had been threatened.

All legal action around the Kent State shootings ended in January 1979 with a $675,000 settlement for the victims. The National Guard signed a statement of regret but emphasized the fact that it was not an apology. The memory of the four students continues to endure, far beyond the borders of Ohio.

A People Walled In

A symbol of suffocating Communist rule, the Berlin Wall stood for more than 20 years.

In the closing days of World War II, conflict ensued over the division of the defeated country of Germany. The four Allied countries of France, Great Britain, the United States, and the Soviet Union originally agreed to share the caretaking of Germany equally. Plans were also made to split the capital of Berlin into eastern and western halves.

EAST VERSUS WEST

The division of Berlin quickly led to cities with clearly different economic and political structures. While West Berlin became a free and democratic economy of "haves," East Berlin adopted a planned financial system based on a Soviet-style government that left them as "have nots."

Many East Berliners envied the wealth and success of West Berliners. By 1961, thousands of East Germans had poured across the border into West Berlin to work, visit, and live. What's more, the open boundary provided access to a free Europe and beyond.

Walter Ulbricht, the East German leader (along with Soviet premier Nikita Khrushchev) was not happy with this coming and going; soon a wall of barbed wire was proposed to restrict free and easy travel. To the satisfaction of the East and the concern of the West, nearly 28 miles of wire fence were erected in August 1961. Eventually, chain-link fencing, booby traps, and armed guards marked the entire border between East and West Germany.

Within a year, a second fence of barbed wire was built nearly 300 feet from the first, creating a "no-man's-land" to discourage any attempts at defecting. Once the original fence went up, the first successful escape was pulled off within two days—ironically, by an East German border guard.

CEMENTING THE HOSTILITIES

By 1965, the East Germans had replaced the barbed-wire fence with an enormous concrete barrier. By 1975, it stood 12 feet high and 4 feet thick and was topped with barbed wire and a rounded pipe to discourage any escapes. More than 300 watchtowers were spaced along the wall, offering armed East German guards a clear and unobstructed view of the "death strip" between the barriers.

The Berlin Wall kept East and West German citizens in their respective "backyards." Allied and Soviet personnel, however, could cross the border at certain passage areas called "checkpoints." The most famous Allied station was known as "Checkpoint Charlie," located halfway along the border, where Allied personnel and foreign travelers crossed between West and East Berlin. Today, it is part of the Allied Museum in western Berlin.

"TEAR DOWN THIS WALL!"

In June 1987, President Ronald Reagan called for Soviet leader Mikhail Gorbachev to remove the long-standing icon of isolation. It took two and a half years for East German officials to announce that their citizens could openly cross the border. Drunk with freedom, many Germans attacked the wall with sledgehammers, breaking off pieces for posterity.

CHAPTER 4
SITES AND STRUCTURES

A True Pyramid Scheme

The Egyptians built three big pyramids at Giza, Egypt, to bury King Tut and so forth, right? There's actually much more to it.

MASTABAS

One might call mastabas proto-pyramids. The oldest examples date to 3500 B.C., and most resemble large pyramid bases of mud, brick, or stone. A typical mastaba contained artwork, images of the deceased, and—of course—mummified Uncle Kahotep (or whomever).

Throughout and after the pyramid era, mastabas remained the budget mausoleum alternative for moderately affluent Egyptians. Because builders clustered mastabas (as they would later do with pyramids), they are often found in groups.

LET'S STACK THESE...

Our best information dates the earliest step pyramid to around 2630 B.C. at Saqqara, Egypt. The architect Imhotep built mastaba

upon mastaba, fashioning a 200-foot-high pyramid as a mausoleum for Pharaoh Djoser. With its original white limestone facing, Djoser's tomb must have been quite a spectacle when struck by the light of the rising sun.

The new tomb style secured Imhotep's immortality—literally, for the Egyptians deified him, and the Greeks identified him with their healing-god Asklepios. Even today, some consider him a patron saint of civil engineers and architects.

I WANT ONE TOO!

Pyramid mania began. Over the next thousand years or so, Egyptian engineers built several pyramid complexes along the Nile's west bank. The most famous and popular today are those at Giza, but dozens survive. Some are majestic, but many are just mounds. We used to believe pyramids were built under the lash. Modern scholars doubt this, but pyramids were definitely huge projects. Some took decades to finish.

The foundation of each pyramid is carved into the bedrock, making the pyramid extremely stable. The Egyptians would do much of the construction work during the Nile's flood season. This way, huge limestone blocks could be floated from the quarries right to the building site. The blocks would then be transported up ramps using ropes made of papyrus twine.

Later, during Roman times, Egypt's neighbor Nubia had a pyramid-building phase. The workmanship and beauty of the Nubian pyramids impress visitors to this day.

WHAT'S INSIDE A PYRAMID?

Stone, mostly. They aren't hollow. Long walkways angle down and up to burial chambers. Narrow shafts extend from these chambers and walkways to vent air out the upper exterior. Most contain painting and writing that has taught us much about Egyptian life; those that were not looted have yielded fabulous artifacts. The burial chambers housed the mummified deceased, of course, with his or her innards in jars nearby.

WHY BUILD THEM?

The Egyptians didn't have a separate word for religion; it touched all aspects of their daily lives. The Pharaoh was a semidivine figure, and a massive Pharaonic tomb represented immense faith and devotion. Egyptians believed that after a Pharaoh died, he would reach the heavens via sunbeams. Egyptians also believed that the pyramid shape would help the Pharaoh on this journey.

Once the Pharaoh reached the heavens, he would become Osiris, the god of the dead. To adequately perform the duties of Osiris, the Pharaoh would need a well-preserved body and organs. The Egyptians feared that if they did not prepare the Pharaoh's body for the afterlife, disaster would fall upon Egypt.

The Egyptians carefully wrapped and mummified the Pharaoh's remains, which was a time-intensive process. They removed and placed the organs in canopic jars because they believed that a different god would watch over each organ. The heart was left in the Pharaoh's body because the Egyptians believed that—as the seat of intelligence and emotions—the Pharaoh would need his heart in the afterlife. The tomb itself was intended to protect the sacred remains and prized possessions.

WHY STOP?

Well, building pyramids required a lot of resources. Worse yet, looters were a constant menace. All that expense and effort, and some jerk breaks in anyway? Some people have no respect!

After about 1800 B.C., the Egyptian art of pyramid construction declined in step with the gradual eclipse of Egypt.

9 Structures That Define America

The United States has a penchant for building. As such, there are numerous buildings and other structures that represent the freedom and opportunity expressed in the American dream. Here are a few of those defining monuments.

1. White House: The history of the White House began when President George Washington and city planner Pierre-Charles L'Enfant chose the site for the presidential residence. Irish-born architect James Hoban's design was chosen in a competition to find a builder of the "President's House." Construction began in October 1792. Although Washington oversaw the building of the house, he never lived in it. When the White House was completed in 1800, President John Adams and his wife, Abigail, moved in as the first residents. Since then, many presidents have made changes and additions. The White House survived a fire at the hands of the British during the War of 1812 and another blaze in the West Wing

in 1929. President Harry Truman gutted and renovated the building during his time there. Encompassing approximately 55,000 square feet, the White House has 6 levels and 132 rooms, including 35 bathrooms. It is the world's only private residence of a head of state that is open to the public.

2. Brooklyn Bridge: Every day, thousands of commuters cross the East River via the Brooklyn Bridge, and they have John A. Roebling and his son, Washington, to thank. In 1867, the elder Roebling was hired as chief engineer to build "the greatest bridge in existence"; he died before construction began, however. Washington stepped in, and construction began in January 1870. The 85-foot-wide bridge was the first steel wire suspension bridge and the largest suspension bridge in the world at the time. On May 24, 1883, the bridge opened to the public, carrying pedestrians, livestock, and trolley cars between Manhattan and Brooklyn. The pedestrian toll that day was a penny but was raised to three cents the next morning. Today, the bridge carries upwards of 144,000 vehicles a day in six lanes of traffic. About 2,000 pedestrians and hundreds of bicyclists also cross the bridge's 1.14 miles each workday.

3. Washington Monument: The Washington Monument, a 555-foot-high white obelisk situated at the west end of the National Mall in Washington, D.C., honors George Washington, Revolutionary War hero and the first president of the United States. Comprised of 36,491 marble, granite, and sandstone blocks, the structure was designed by Robert Mills. Construction began in 1848, but due to the outbreak of the Civil War and lack of funding, it took nearly 40 years to complete. It is clearly visible where work resumed in 1876 by the difference in the marble's shading, about 150 feet up the obelisk. The monument was dedicated in 1885 but did not officially open to the public until October 9, 1888, after the internal construction was complete. At the time it was the world's tallest structure.

4. Lincoln Memorial: "In this temple, as in the hearts of the people for whom he saved the Union, the memory of Abraham Lincoln is enshrined forever." These words are inscribed at the top of the Lincoln Memorial. Designed by architect Henry Bacon, sculptor Daniel Chester French, and artist Jules Guerin, the structure was completed in 1922. The monument is ringed by 36 columns, one for each state in the Union (at the time of Lincoln's death). Seated within the monument is a sculpture of Lincoln, and inscriptions from both the Gettysburg Address and his second inaugural address adorn the walls.

5. Empire State Building: The Empire State Building is a crown jewel of the New York City skyline. Designed by William Lamb, the structure was the world's tallest building when it opened in 1931. More than 3,000 workers took fewer than 14 months to build the structure, with the framework erected at a pace of 4.5 stories per week. On a clear day the observatory offers glimpses of the five surrounding states.

6. Golden Gate Bridge: San Francisco's Golden Gate Bridge was the vision of chief engineer Joseph B. Strauss, whose contemporaries maintained that such a bridge could not be built. Nevertheless, construction began on January 5, 1933. Nearly four and a half years, $35 million, and 11 worker fatalities later, the bridge was opened to an estimated 200,000 pedestrians on May 27, 1937, and to vehicles the next day. The bridge is 1.7 miles long and 90 feet wide. The bridge has two principal cables passing over the tops of the two main towers. If laid end to end, the total length of wire in both main cables would total 80,000 miles. The Golden Gate Bridge is painted "International Orange," making it more visible to ships and the 38 million vehicles that cross it annually in the lingering and persistent fog.

7. St. Louis Arch: The St. Louis Arch on the bank of the Mississippi River marks the city as the "Gateway to the West." Thomas Jefferson's vision of freedom and democracy spreading from "sea to shining sea" inspired architect Eero Saarinen's contemporary design for a 630-foot stainless steel memorial. Construction began in 1963 and was completed on October 28, 1965. The Arch's foundation is set 60 feet into the ground and is built to withstand earthquakes and high winds. A 40-passenger train takes sightseers from the lobby to the observation platform, where on a clear day the view stretches for 30 miles.

8. Statue of Liberty: The Statue of Liberty is perhaps the most enduring symbol of America and has become a universal symbol of freedom and democracy. Located on a 12-acre island in New York Harbor, the Statue of Liberty was a friendly gesture from the people of France to the people of the United States. The statue, designed by French sculptor Frédéric Auguste Bartholdi, was dedicated on October 28, 1886, designated a national monument in 1924, and underwent a face-lift for its centennial in 1986. Lady Liberty stands 305 feet 1 inch high, from the ground to the tip of her torch.

9. Vietnam Veterans Memorial: This memorial in Washington, D.C., honors the men and women who served in one of America's most divisive wars. The memorial was intended to heal the nation's emotional wounds and was designed to be neutral about the war itself. Three components comprise the memorial: the Wall of Names, the Three Servicemen Statue and Flagpole, and the Vietnam Women's Memorial. The Wall was built in 1982 and designed by Maya Lin. Visitors descend a path along two walls of black granite with one wing pointing at the Washington Monument a mile away and the other at the Lincoln Memorial about 600 feet away. The names of

59,000 soldiers killed or missing in action dominate the Vietnam Veterans Memorial.

Sandstone Gateway to Heaven

For hundreds of years, rumors of the lost city of Angkor spread among Cambodian peasants. On a stifling day in 1860, Henri Mahout and his porters discovered that the ancient city was more than mere legend.

French botanist and explorer Henri Mahout wiped his spectacles as he pushed into a Cambodian jungle clearing. Gasping for breath in the thick mists, he gazed down weed-ridden avenues at massive towers and stone temples wreathed with carvings of gods, kings, and battles. The ruins before him were none other than the temples of Angkor Wat.

Although often credited with the discovery of Angkor Wat, Mahout was not the first Westerner to encounter the site. He did, however, bring the "lost" city to the attention of the European public when his travel journals were published in 1868. He wrote: "One of these temples—a rival to that of Solomon, and erected by some ancient Michelangelo—might take an honorable place beside our most beautiful buildings."

Mahout's descriptions of this massive unexplored Hindu temple sent a jolt of lightning through academic circles. Explorers combed the jungles of northern Cambodia in an attempt to explain the meaning and origin of the mysterious lost shrine.

THE RISE OF THE KHMER

Scholars first theorized that Angkor Wat and other ancient temples in present-day Cambodia were about

2,000 years old. However, as they began to decipher the Sanskrit inscriptions, they found that the temples had been erected during the 9th through 12th centuries. While Europe languished in the Dark Ages, the Khmer Empire of Indochina was reaching its zenith.

The earliest records of the Khmer people date to the middle of the 6th century. They migrated from southern China and Tibet and settled in what is now Cambodia. The early Khmer retained many Indian influences—they were Hindus, and their architecture evolved from Indian building methods.

In the early 9th century, King Jayavarman II laid claim to an independent kingdom called Kambuja. He established his capital some 190 miles north of Phnom Penh, the modern Cambodian capital. Jayavarman II also introduced the cult of *devaraja*, which claimed that the Khmer king was a representative of Shiva, the Hindu god of destruction and rebirth. As such, in addition to the temples built to honor the Hindu gods, temples were also constructed to serve as tombs for kings.

The Khmer built more than 100 stone temples spread out over about 40 miles. The temples were made from laterite (a material similar to clay that forms in tropical climates) and sandstone. The sandstone provided an open canvas for the statues and reliefs celebrating the Hindu gods.

HOME OF THE GODS

During the first half of the 12th century, Kambuja's King Suryavarman II decided to raise an enormous temple dedicated to the Hindu god Vishnu, a religious monument that would subdue the surrounding jungle and illustrate the power of the Khmer king. His masterpiece—the largest temple complex in the world—would be known to history by its Sanskrit name, "Angkor Wat," or "City of Temple."

Pilgrims visiting Angkor Wat in the 12th century would enter the temple complex by crossing a square, 600-foot-wide moat that ran some four miles in perimeter around the temple grounds. Approaching from the west, visitors would tread the moat's causeway to the main gateway. From there, they would follow a spiritual journey representing the path from the outside world through the Hindu universe and into Mount Meru, the home of the gods. They would pass a giant statue of an eight-armed Vishnu as they entered the western *gopura*, or gatehouse, known as the "Entrance of the Elephants." They would then follow a stone walkway decorated with *nagas* (mythical serpents) past sunken pools and column-studded buildings once believed to house sacred temple documents.

At the end of the stone walkway, a pilgrim would step up to a platform surrounded with galleries featuring six-foot-high bas-reliefs of gods and kings. One depicts the Churning of the Ocean of Milk, a Hindu story in which gods and demons churn a serpent in an ocean of milk to extract the elixir of life. Another illustrates the epic battle of monkey warriors against demons whose sovereign had kidnapped Sita, the beautiful wife of Rama (the Hindu deity of chivalry and virtue). Others depict the gruesome fates awaiting the wicked in the afterlife.

A visitor to King Suryavarman's kingdom would next ascend the dangerously steep steps to the temple's second level, an enclosed area boasting a courtyard decorated with hundreds of dancing *apsaras*, female images ornamented with jewelry and elaborately dressed hair.

For kings and high priests, the journey would continue with a climb up more steep steps to a 126-foot-high central temple, the pinnacle of Khmer society. Spreading out some 145 feet on each side, the square temple includes a courtyard cornered by four high conical towers shaped to look like lotus buds. The center of the temple is dominated by a fifth conical tower soaring 180 feet above the main causeway; inside it holds a golden statue of the Khmer patron, Vishnu, riding a half-man, half-bird creature in the image of King Suryavarman.

DISUSE AND DESTRUCTION

With the decline of the Khmer Empire and the resurgence of Buddhism, Angkor Wat was occupied by Buddhist monks for many years. A cruciform gallery leading to the temple's second level was decorated with 1,000 Buddhas; the Vishnu statue in the central tower was replaced by an image of Buddha. The temple fell into various states of disrepair over the centuries and is now the focus of international restoration efforts.

The Mystery of Easter Island

On Easter Sunday in 1722, a Dutch ship landed on a small island 2,300 miles from the coast of South America. Polynesian explorers had preceded them by a thousand years or more, and the Europeans found the descendants of those early visitors still living on the island. They also found a strange collection of almost 900 enormous stone heads, or *moai*, standing with their backs to the sea, gazing across the island with eyes hewn out of coral. The image of those faces haunts visitors to this day.

ANCESTORS AT THE END OF THE LAND

Easter Island legend tells of the great Chief Hotu Matu'a, the Great Parent, striking out from Polynesia in a canoe, taking his family on a voyage across the trackless ocean in search of a new home. He made landfall on Te-Pito-te-Henua, the End of the Land, sometime between A.D. 400 and 700. Finding the island well-suited to habitation, his descendants spread out to cover much of it, living off the natural bounty of the land and sea. With their survival assured, they built *ahu*—ceremonial sites featuring a large stone mound—and on them erected *moai*, which were representations of notable chieftains who led the island over the centuries. The *moai* weren't literal depictions of their ancestors, but rather embodied their spirit, or *mana*, and conferred blessings and protection on the islanders.

The construction of these *moai* was quite a project. A hereditary class of sculptors oversaw the main quarry, located near one of the volcanic mountains on the island. Groups of people would request a *moai* for their local *ahu*, and the sculptors would go to work, their efforts supported by gifts of food and other goods. Over time, they created 887 of the stone *moai*, averaging just over 13 feet tall and weighing around 14 tons, but ranging from one extreme of just under four feet tall to a behemoth that towered 71 feet. The *moai* were then transported across the island by a mechanism that still remains in doubt, but that may have involved rolling them on the trunks of palm trees felled for that purpose—a technique that was to have terrible repercussions for the islanders.

When Europeans first made landfall on Easter Island, they found an island full of standing *moai*. Fifty-two years later, James Cook reported that many of the statues had been toppled, and by the 1830s none were left standing. What's more, the statues hadn't just been knocked over; many of them had boulders placed at strategic locations, with the intention of decapitating the *moai* when they were pulled down. What happened?

A CULTURE ON THE BRINK

The original Dutch explorers had encountered a culture on the rebound. At the time of their arrival, they found two or three thousand living on the island, but some estimates put the population as high as fifteen thousand a century before. The story of the islanders' decline is one in which many authors find a cautionary tale: The people simply consumed natural resources to the point where their land could no longer support them.

By the 1600s, life had changed: The last forests on the island disappeared, and the islanders' traditional foodstuffs vanished from the archaeological record. Local tradition tells of a time of famine and even rumored cannibalism, and it is from this time that island history reveals the appearance of the spear. Tellingly, the Polynesian words for "wood" begin to take on a connotation of wealth, a meaning found nowhere else that shares the language.

Perhaps worst of all, with their forests gone, the islanders had no material to make the canoes that would have allowed them to leave their island in search of resources. They were trapped, and they turned on one another.

The Europeans found a reduced society that had just emerged from this time of terror. The respite was short-lived, however. The arrival of the foreigners seems to have come at a critical moment in the history of Easter Island.

Either coincidentally or spurred on by the strangers, a warrior class seized power across the island, and different groups vied for power. Villages were burned, their resources taken by the victors, and the defeated left to starve. The warfare also led to the toppling of an enemy's *moai*—whether to capture their *mana* or simply prevent it from being used against the opposing faction.

In the end, none of the *moai* remained standing.

DOWNFALL AND REBOUND

The troubles of Easter Island weren't limited to self-inflicted chaos. The arrival of the white man also introduced smallpox and syphilis; the islanders, with little natural immunity to the exotic diseases, fared no better than native populations elsewhere on the planet.

As if that weren't enough, other ships arrived, collecting slaves for work in South America. The internal fighting and external pressure combined to reduce the number of native islanders to little more than a hundred by 1877—the last survivors of a people who once enjoyed a tropical paradise.

Easter Island, or Rapa Nui, was annexed by Chile in 1888. According to a 2017 census, there are 7,750 people living on the island. There are projects under way to raise the fallen *moai*. Approximately 50 have been returned to their former glory.

Then and Now: Ancient Cities

In the ancient world, it took far fewer people to make a great city. Some didn't survive, but others have flourished. With the understanding that ancient population estimates are necessarily approximate, here are the fates of some great metropolises:

◈ **Memphis (now the ruins of Memphis, Egypt):** By 3100 B.C., this Pharaonic capital bustled with an estimated 30,000 people. Today it has none—but modern Cairo, 12 miles north, is home to an estimated 19 million people.

◈ **Ur (now the ruins of Ur, Iraq):** Sumer's great ancient city once stood near the Euphrates with a peak population of 65,000 around 2030 B.C. The Euphrates has meandered about ten miles northeast, and Ur now has a population of zero.

◈ **Alexandria (now El-Iskandariya, Egypt):** Built on an ancient Egyptian village site near the Nile Delta's west end, Alexander the Great's city once held a tremendous library. In its heyday, it may have held 250,000 people; today an estimated 5.2 million people call it home.

◈ **Babylon (now the ruins of Babylon, Iraq):** Babylon may have twice been the largest city in the world, in about 1700 B.C. and 500 B.C.—perhaps with up to 200,000 people in the latter case. Now, it's windblown dust and faded splendor.

◈ **Athens (Greece):** In classical times, this powerful city-state stood miles from the coast but was never a big place—something like 30,000 residents during the 300s B.C. It now reaches the sea with about 3 million residents.

◈ **Rome (Italy):** With the rise of its empire, ancient Rome became a city of more than 500,000 and the center of Western civilization. Though that mantle moved on to other cities, Rome now has around 2.8 million people.

◈ **Xi'an (China):** This longtime dynastic capital, famed for its terra-cotta warriors but home to numerous other antiquities, reached 400,000 people by A.D. 637. Its nearly 8 million people make it as important a city now as then.

◈ **Constantinople (now Istanbul, Turkey):** First colonized by Greeks in the 1200s B.C., this city of fame was made Emperor Constantine the Great's eastern imperial Roman capital with 300,000 people. As Byzantium, it bobbed and wove through the tides of faith and conquest. Today, it is Turkey's largest city with around 15 million people.

◈ **Baghdad (Iraq):** Founded around A.D. 762, this center of Islamic culture and faith was perhaps the first city to house more than 1,000,000 people. It has sometimes faded but never fallen.

◈ **Tenochtitlán (now Mexico City, Mexico):** Founded in A.D. 1325, this island-built Aztec capital had more than 200,000 inhabitants within a century. Most of the surrounding lake has been drained over the years. Today, a staggering 21 million souls call modern Mexico City home.

◈ **Carthage (now the ruins of Carthage, Tunisia):** Phoenician seafarers from the Levant founded this great trade city in 814 B.C. Before the Romans obliterated it in 146 B.C., its population may have reached 700,000. Today, it sits in empty silence ten miles from modern Tunis—population 2.2 million.

Red City of the Nabataeans

In the wilds of southern Jordan lies one of antiquity's most beautifully preserved sights.

Where exactly is Petra?
Petra is a city within the Hashemite Kingdom of Jordan, perhaps 80 miles south of Amman in the Naqab (Negev) Desert, about 15 miles east of the Israeli border. It is a World Heritage Site and a Jordanian national treasure, cared for accordingly.

Why settle out in the desert?
Petra was a key link in the trade chain connecting Egypt, Babylon, Arabia, and the Mediterranean. It had water (if you knew how to look) and was quite defensible.

When was it founded?
In 600 B.C., the narrow red sandstone canyon of Petra housed a settlement of Edomites: seminomadic Semites said to descend from the biblical Esau. Egypt was still rich but declining. Rome was a young farming community dominated by its Etruscan kings. The rise of classical Athens was decades away. Brutal Assyria had fallen to Babylonian conquerors. With the rise of the incense trade, Arab traders began pitching tents at what would become Petra. We know them as the Nabataeans.

Did they speak Arabic?
Nabataean history spanned a millennium. They showed up speaking early Arabic in a region where Aramaic was the business-speak. The newcomers thus first wrote their Arabic in a variant of the Aramaic script. But Petra's trade focus meant a need to adopt Aramaic as well, so Nabataeans did. By the end (about 250 years before the rise of Islam), Nabataean "Arabaic" had evolved into classical (Koranic) Arabic.

What were these Nabataeans like?

The Swiss or Swedes of the biblical world. They weren't expansionists, but defended their homeland with shrewd diplomacy and obstinate vigor. Despite great wealth, they had few slaves. Despite monarchical government, Petra's Nabataeans showed a pronounced democratic streak. Empires rose and fell around them; business was business.

The trade must have been lucrative indeed.

Vastly. The core commodity was incense from Arabia, but many raw materials and luxuries of antiquity also passed through Petra—notably bitumen (natural asphalt), useful in waterproofing and possibly in embalming.

Speaking of religion, were they religious?

Religious, yes; fanatical, no. Most Nabataeans were pagan, worshipping benevolent fertility and sun deities. Jews were welcome at Petra, as were Christians in its later days.

What of Nabataean women's roles?

Nabataean women held a respected position in society, including property and inheritance rights. While no major ancient Near Eastern culture was truly egalitarian, the women of Petra participated in its luxuriant prosperity.

Take me to Petra in its heyday. What do I experience?

It is 70 B.C., and you walk the streets of Petra, home to about 20,000 people. Ornate homes and public buildings rivaling Athenian and Roman artistry are carved into the high red sandstone walls of the canyon. A camel caravan arrives from Arabia loaded with goods; white-robed traders dismount with elegant gifts for their buying contacts. The wealthy aroma of frankincense constantly reminds your nostrils why Petra exists. Most people wear robes and cloaks, often colored by exotic dyes. Petra is luxurious without being licentious.

You overhear conversations in Aramaic and Arabic: A new cistern is under construction. Workers are shoring up a building damaged by a recent earth tremor. Old-timers grouse that reigning King Aretas III wishes he were Greek. A modestly robed vendor walks past with dates for sale; you fish out a thick silver coin to offer her. Along with your bronze change and the delicious dates, she wishes you the favor of al-Uzza, the Nabataean goddess identified with Aphrodite and Venus.

You ask a passing water-bearer: Who's that guy in the outlandish robe draped over one shoulder, followed by servants? A man of faraway Rome, says she. You've heard of this Rome, a dynamic market for Petra's goods, with domains beginning to rival Alexander the Great's once-mighty empire. Only time will tell how Petra will reckon with this next tide of power.

No one lives at Petra now. When and why did it decline?

Petra's last king, Rabbel II, willed his realm to Rome. When he died in A.D. 106, Nabataea became the Roman province of Arabia Petraea. Again the Nabataeans adjusted—and kept up the trade. In the 2nd and 3rd centuries A.D., the caravans began using Palmyra (in modern Syria) as an alternate route, starting a slow decline at Petra. An earthquake in 363 delivered the knockout punch: damage to the intricate water system sustaining the city. By about 400, Petra was an Arabian ghost town.

How might I see this for myself?

Thousands do it daily. If you can travel to Jordan, you can travel to Petra—either with an organized tour booked through a travel agent or on your own if that's your style. Nearby hotels and restaurants offer modern accommodations. The site charges a daily entrance fee.

The Mound Builders: Mythmaking in Early America

The search for an improbable past—or how to make a mountain out of a molehill.

In the early 1840s, the fledgling United States was gripped by a controversy that spilled from the parlors of the educated men in Boston and Philadelphia—the core of the nation's intellectual elite—onto the pages of the newspapers printed for mass edification. In the tiny farming village of Grave Creek, Virginia (now West Virginia), on the banks of the Ohio River, stood one of the largest earthen mounds discovered during white man's progress westward. The existence of these mounds, spread liberally throughout the Mississippi Valley, Ohio River Valley, and much of the southeast, was commonly known and had caused a great deal of speculative excitement since Europeans had first arrived on the continent. Hernando de Soto, for one, had mentioned the mounds of the Southeast during his wandering in that region.

MONEY WELL SPENT

The colonists who settled the East Coast noticed that the mounds, which came in a variety of sizes and shapes, were typically placed near excellent sites for villages and farms. The Grave Creek mound was among the first of the major earthworks discovered by white men in their westward expansion. By 1838, the property was owned and farmed by the Tomlinson family.

Abelard B. Tomlinson took an interest in the mound on his family's land and decided to open a vertical shaft from its summit, 70 feet high, to the center. He discovered skeletal remains at various levels and a timbered vault at the base containing the remains of two individuals. More importantly, he discovered a sandstone tablet inscribed with three lines of characters of unknown origin.

WHO WERE THE BUILDERS?

Owing to the general belief that the aborigines were lazy and incapable of such large operations—and the fact that none of the tribes who dwelt near the mounds claimed any knowledge of who had built them—many 19th-century Americans believed that the mound builders could not have been the ancestors of the Native American tribes they encountered. By the early 19th century, the average American assumed that the mound builders had been a pre-Columbian expedition from the Old World—Vikings, Israelites, refugees from Atlantis—all these and more had their champions. Most agreed, however, that the New World had once hosted and given rise to a civilization as advanced as that of the Aztecs and Incas who had then fallen into disarray or been conquered by the savage barbarians that now inhabited the land. Speculation on the history of the mound builders led many, including Thomas Jefferson, to visit the mounds and conduct their own studies.

MORMONS AND THE MOUNDS

Meanwhile, the Grave Creek tablet fanned the flames of a controversy that was roaring over the newly established—and widely despised—Church of Jesus Christ of Latter-day Saints. The religion is based upon the belief that the American continent was once inhabited by lost tribes of Israel who divided into warring factions and fought each other to near extinction. The last surviving prophet of these people, Mormon, inscribed his people's history upon gold tablets, which were interred in a mound near present-day Palmyra, New York, until they were revealed to fifteen-year-old Joseph Smith in 1823.

Though many Americans were ready to believe that the mounds represented the remains of a nonaboriginal culture, they were less ready to believe in Smith's new religion. Smith and his adherents were persecuted horribly, and Smith was killed by an angry mob while leading his followers west. Critics of the Latter-day Saints (as the Mormons prefer to be called) point to the early 19th-century publication of several popular books purporting that the earthen mounds of North America were the remains of lost tribes of Israel. These texts claimed that evidence would eventually be discovered to support their author's assertions. That the young Smith should have his revelation so soon after these fanciful studies were published struck many observers as entirely too coincidental. Thus, Abelard Tomlinson's excavation of the sandstone tablet with its strange figures ignited the passions of both Smith's followers and his detractors.

ENTER THE SCHOLAR

Into this theological, and ultimately anthropological, maelstrom strode Henry Rowe Schoolcraft, a mineralogist whose keen interest in Native American history had led to his appointment as head of Indian affairs. While working in Sault Ste. Marie, Michigan, Schoolcraft married a native woman and mastered the Ojibwa language. Schoolcraft traveled to Grave Creek to examine Tomlinson's tablet and concluded that the figures were indeed a language but deferred to more learned scholars to determine just which language they represented. The opinions were many and varied—from Celtic runes to early Greek; experts the world over weighed in with their opinions. Nevertheless, Schoolcraft was more concerned with physical evidence and close study of the mounds themselves, and he remained convinced that the mounds and the artifacts they carried were the products of ancestors of the Native Americans. Schoolcraft's theory flew in the face of both those who sought to defend and those who sought to debunk the Mormon belief, and it would be more than three decades until serious scholarship and the emergence of true archaeological techniques began to shift opinion on the subject.

ANSWERS PROPOSED, BUT QUESTIONS STILL ABOUND

History has vindicated Schoolcraft's careful and thoughtful study of the mounds. Today, we know that the mound builders were not descendants of Israel, nor were they the offspring of Vikings. They were simply the ancient and more numerous predecessors of the Native Americans, who constructed the mounds for protection from floods and as burial sites, temples, and defense strongholds. As for the Grave Creek tablet: Scholars today generally agree that the figures are not a written language but simply a fanciful design whose meaning, if ever there was one, has been lost to the ages. Though the Smithsonian Institution has several etchings of the tablet in its collection, the whereabouts of the actual tablet have been lost to the ages.

Seven Wonders of the Ancient World

It was the ultimate destination guide—seven of the most spectacular hand-built wonders of the world. In fact, the Greek referred to these wonders as *theamati*, which translates roughly to "must-sees."

The first comprehensive listing of the Seven Wonders has been attributed to Herodotus, a Greek historian dating back to the 5th century B.C. Other versions soon followed—each reflecting the writer's opinion of what was worth mentioning and often naming many more than seven sights.

Most of the earliest lists were lost; the oldest existing version known today was compiled by Antipater of Sidon in 140 B.C. The items on his list, with a few revisions, are the ones that came to forever be known as the Seven Wonders of the Ancient World. Unfortunately, only one of the seven still exists today; all that remains of the other six are descriptions from writers over the centuries.

SO WHAT'S THE BIG DEAL?

What makes the seven wonders so wonderful? It's a combination of factors: the intricacies of the architecture, the scale of engineering, and the beauty of each project—not to mention the construction technology and materials available for use at the time.

Religion often played a big role in the significance of these structures. Some were built to honor certain gods. Others were built to showcase important rulers, a number of whom had achieved a godlike following.

AND THE SEVEN WONDERS ARE...

1. **The Great Pyramid of Giza:** Located on the west bank of the Nile river near Cairo, Egypt, this is the largest of ten pyramids built between 2600 and 2500 B.C. Built for King Khufu, the Great Pyramid was constructed by thousands of workers toiling for nearly a quarter of a century (2609 B.C.–2584 B.C.).

The structure consists of more than two million 2.5-ton stones. If the stones were piled on top of each other, the resulting tower would be close to 50 stories high. The base covers an astonishing 13 acres. It's not known exactly how the blocks were lifted. Theories include mud-

and water-coated ramps or an intricate system of levers. Not only did the blocks have to be lifted, but they also had to be transported from the quarries. Even the experts can't say exactly how that was done. The mystery is part of the fascination.

The pyramid originally stood 481 feet high but has been weathered down to about 450 feet. It was considered the tallest structure on the planet for 43 centuries. The Great Pyramid is the only Wonder of the Ancient World still standing—a testament to one of the mightiest civilizations in history.

2. The Hanging Gardens of Babylon: Legend has it that King Nebuchadnezzar II, ruler of Babylon (near modern Baghdad, Iraq), built the gardens around 600 B.C. as a present for his wife, Amytis of Media. The gardens consisted of a series of terraces holding trees, exotic plants, and shady pools—all fed by water piped in from the Euphrates River and rising about 60 feet high. References to the Gardens appear as late as the first century B.C., after which they disappear from contemporary accounts. There has been some speculation over whether or not the Gardens ever even actually existed.

3. The Temple of Artemis at Ephesus: Constructed around 550 B.C. in what is now Turkey, the Temple was built in honor of Artemis (Diana), goddess of hunting and nature. The marble temple measured 377 by 180 feet and had a tile-covered roof held up by at least 106 columns between 40 and 60 feet high. The temple held priceless art and also functioned as the treasury of the city. It stood until 356 B.C. when it was purposely destroyed by an artist, known in infamy as Herostratus, who burned the Temple merely so his name would be remembered for ages. The outraged Ephesians rebuilt the temple, this time entirely of stone, but the new building was destroyed by invading Goths in A.D. 262. A few surviving sculptures are displayed at the British Museum.

4. The Statue of Zeus at Olympia: Even contemporary historians and archaeologists consider the Statue of Zeus at Olympia to be one of the best-known statues in the ancient world. The image, standing 40 feet high with a 20-foot base, was constructed by Phidias around 435 B.C. to honor Zeus, king of the gods. The statue depicted a seated Zeus (made of ivory, though his robes and sandals were made of gold) holding a golden figure of the goddess of victory in one hand and a staff topped with an eagle in the other. Atop his head was a wreath of olive branches.

In the flickering lamplight of the temple, the statue seemed almost alive and attracted pilgrims from all over Greece for eight centuries. After the old gods were outlawed by Christian emperor Theodosius, the statue was taken as a prize to Constantinople, where it was destroyed in a fire around A.D. 462.

5. The Mausoleum of Maussollos: This white marble tomb, built in what is today southwestern Turkey, was built around 353 B.C. for Maussollos, a Persian king. Around 45 stories tall, the building was covered in relief sculpture depicting scenes from mythology; gaps were filled in with bigger-than-life statues of famous heroes and gods. The very top was capped with a marble statue of Maussollos, pulled in a chariot by four horses. The structure was so impressive that the king's name has been lent to the present-day word *mausoleum*, now used to refer to an impressive burial place.

The tomb remained largely intact until the 13th century, when it was severely damaged by a series of earthquakes. In 1494, the Knights of Saint John raided its stonework to use as building materials for a castle being constructed nearby, and thus the Mausoleum was lost to history.

6. The Colossus of Rhodes: Standing nearly 110 feet tall—rivaling the modern Statue of Liberty, which tops out at 151 feet—the Colossus of Rhodes was a sight to behold. The bronze statue was built near the harbor of Rhodes in the Aegean Sea in honor of the sun god Helios. Construction took 12 years—from approximately 292 B.C. to 280 B.C. The exact pose of the statue is a matter of debate; records say that one arm was raised but are maddeningly silent on other details. The statue stood for only 56 years before it was toppled by an earthquake. It lay on the ground for another 800 years, still a tourist attraction. Accounts say a popular tourist game was to see if a person could encircle one of the fallen statue's thumbs with their arms. Finally, in A.D. 654, Rhodes was captured by Arab invaders who broke up the statue and melted it down for its bronze.

7. The Lighthouse of Alexandria: The youngest of the ancient wonders was a building with a civic, rather than a spiritual, purpose. The famed lighthouse of Alexandria was built around 250 B.C. to aid ships making the journey into that city's harbor. At 380 feet tall, it was a marvel of ancient engineering. Overshadowed only by the two tallest Egyptian pyramids, a tower of greater height wouldn't be constructed for centuries. An interior ramp led up to a platform supporting a series of polished bronze mirrors, which would reflect sunlight during the day and firelight at night. The fuel source is uncertain but may have been oil or even animal dung. Some accounts claim the lighthouse could be seen 300 miles from the shore; this is almost certainly exaggerated, but more reasonable claims of 35 miles are impressive enough. The lighthouse was destroyed by an earthquake in the 1300s.

LEGACY

It is a tribute to our ancestors that they were able to create works of architecture that capture our imagination even thousands of years after the structures themselves were destroyed. Several efforts are under way to name a definitive list of modern wonders, with such candidates as the Eiffel Tower and the Golden Gate Bridge. One such effort elicited votes from people all over the world via the Internet. The resulting list of the "New 7 Wonders of the World" was released in July 2007. The finalists, in no particular order, are: Petra, Jordan; the Great Wall of China; the Christ Redeemer, Brazil; the Taj Majal, India; Chichén Itzá, Mexico; the Colosseum, Italy; and Machu Picchu, Peru.

CHAPTER 5

TOWERING FIGURES

Julius Caesar: Oppressor or Enlightened Leader?

Julius Caesar is one of the most recognized figures in all of human history. However, most people don't know as much about him as they think.

Caesar was not the first Roman emperor; indeed, he was never an emperor at all. He was a dictator, but in his time that word had a reasonable and legitimate political connotation. As history suggests, Caesar was capable in many areas. He led men into battle with courage and skill and was also a brilliant administrator and politician who instituted reforms that benefited most Romans.

RISING OUT OF CHAOS

Caesar's birth in 100 B.C. coincided with great civil strife in Rome. Although his parents' status as nobles gave him advantages, Caesar's childhood was volatile. As an adult, he learned to be wary in his dealings with others. By the time Caesar was 20, a patrician named Sulla had been the Roman dictator for about 20 years. Although Caesar and Sulla were friends, Sulla later became enraged when Caesar refused to divorce his wife, Cornelia, who was the daughter of Cinna, a man Sulla loathed. To save his neck, Caesar promptly left for Asia.

When Sulla died in 78 B.C., Caesar returned to Rome and took up the practice of law. Caesar had everything necessary for success: He had received the best possible education, developed impressive oratorical skills, and was an outstanding writer. He also spent huge sums of money, most of which he had to borrow. The money went to bribes and sumptuous parties and bought Caesar access to power. Leading politicians looked on him favorably and rewarded him with a series of increasingly important political positions in Spain and Rome. Caesar's time in Spain was especially useful, as he used his position there to become very wealthy.

COMING OUT ON TOP

In 59 B.C., Caesar, who was by now a general, made a successful bid for power in concert with Marcus Licinius Crassus, the richest man in Rome; and Pompey, another ambitious general who was known, to his immodest pleasure, as Pompey the Great. These three Type-A personalities ruled Rome as the First Triumvirate, with Caesar becoming first among equals as consul. Caesar had always been popular among the common people and with Rome's soldiers, and he aimed to cement that loyalty with reforms that would benefit them. Soon, Caesar was made governor of Gaul and spent the next 11 years conquering all of what is now France, with a couple of profitable trips to Britain for good measure. While on campaign, he wrote an account of his actions, called *Commentaries*, which is among the finest of all military literature.

OLD FRIENDS AND NEW

To leave Rome, even for military glory, was always risky for any of the empire's leaders. While Caesar was abroad, Crassus was killed in battle. This void encouraged Pompey, who made it clear that Caesar was no longer welcome in Rome. Caesar and his army responded by crossing the Rubicon River in 49 B.C. to seize control of the city. Within a year of the civil war that followed, Caesar defeated Pompey. He also began a torrid affair with Egypt's Queen Cleopatra. After a few other actions against Rome's enemies, Caesar was acclaimed by all of Rome as a great hero. In turn, he pardoned all who had opposed him.

HAIL, CAESAR

Mindful of the fleeting nature of popularity, Caesar continued to promote a series of important reforms:

◈ Some of the land that had been held by wealthy families was distributed to common people desperate to make a living. As one might expect, this didn't go over well with the wealthy.

◈ Tax reforms insisted upon by Caesar forced the rich to pay their fair share. This innovation didn't win Caesar many new friends among the powerful.

◈ Retired soldiers were settled on land provided by the government. Because this land was in Rome's outlying territories, it became populated with a happy, well-trained cadre of veterans meant to be Rome's first line of defense, if needed. Unemployed citizens were also given the opportunity to settle in these areas, where jobs were much more plentiful. This reduced the number of poor people in Rome and decreased the crime rate.

◈ As he had done earlier, Caesar made residents of the provinces, such as people living in Spain, citizens of Rome. This idea proved quite popular. Many years later, some of the Roman emperors actually came from Spain.

◆ Working people are happy people (so it's said). In a clever move, Caesar instituted a massive public works program that provided both jobs and a sense of pride among the citizens of Rome.

BEWARE THE IDES OF MARCH

All these reforms notwithstanding, Caesar's enemies feared he would leverage his great popularity to destroy the Roman Republic and institute in its place an empire ruled by one man. So, in one of those moments of violence that turns the wheel of history, Caesar was assassinated on March 15, 44 B.C.—the Ides of March, for those of you who remember your Shakespeare. The civil war that followed was ultimately won by Caesar's nephew, Octavian, who changed his name to Caesar Augustus . . . and who replaced the republic and instituted in its place an empire ruled by one man! Augustus was the first of a long succession of emperors who ruled virtually independent of the Roman Senate. It was the rulers who followed Caesar, then, and not Caesar himself, who proved the undoing of the system so cherished by Caesar's enemies.

Awesome Ottoman

Süleyman the Magnificent was a warrior-scholar who lived up to his billing. A Turkish Sultan who reigned from 1520 to 1566, Süleyman led the Ottoman Empire to its greatest heights.

Not only was Süleyman a brilliant military strategist, he was also a great legislator, an impartial ruler, and a devotee of the arts. During his rule, he expanded the country's military empire and brought cultural and architectural projects to new heights. For all this and more, Süleyman is considered one of the finest leaders of 16th-century Europe.

Under Süleyman's leadership, his forces conquered Iraq and successfully occupied it until the First World War. Süleyman annexed or made allies of the Barbary States of North Africa, which remained a thorn in Europe's underbelly until the 1800s. He also led an army that went deep into Europe itself, crushing the Hungarian King Louis II at the great Battle of Mohács in 1526, which led to the Siege of Vienna.

An accomplished poet, Süleyman was gracious in victory, saying of the young Louis: "It was not my wish that he should be thus cut off while he scarcely tasted the sweets of life and royalty." To his favorite wife Hurrem, a harem woman and daughter of a Ukrainian Orthodox priest, he wrote: "My springtime, my merry faced love, my daytime, my sweetheart, laughing leaf . . . My woman of the beautiful hair, my love of the slanted brow, my love of eyes full of mischief . . ."

While Shari'ah, or sacred law, ruled his far-flung land's religious life, Süleyman reformed the Ottomans' civil law code. In fact, the Ottomans called him Kanuni, or "The Lawgiver." The final form of Süleyman's legal code would remain in place for more than 300 years.

Important People You've Probably Never Heard Of

"Ötzi the Iceman" (ca. 3300 B.C.) was a natural mummy found on the border between Austria and Italy in 1991. This spectacularly preserved specimen of a middle-aged Chalcolithic (Copper Age) European male was popularly named after the Otztal Alps where he was discovered in a glacier. He stood about five feet four inches, weighed about 84 pounds, and boasted 57 tattoos—mostly small lines. Ötzi was amazingly well-equipped for his journey across the mountains: He carried a copper axe with a yew handle, a flint knife, a quiver full of arrows, and an unfinished yew longbow. The pouch on his belt was a combined fire-starting and medicinal kit that contained flint, pyrite, tinder fungus, birch fungus (known to have antibacterial properties), two bark baskets (one containing charcoal), berries, and more than a dozen different plants. His wardrobe consisted of a cloak made of woven grass; a loincloth, leggings, vest, and belt made of leather; a bearskin hat; and waterproof shoes made of bearskin, deer hide, and tree bark, stuffed with grass for warmth. Petr Hlavacek, a Czech footwear expert from Tomas Bata University, re-created Ötzi's shoes using a prehistoric tanning process that involved boiling the liver and brains of pigs. The result, he writes, was "like going barefoot, only better."

Aristarchus of Samos (310 B.C.–230 B.C.) was a Greek astronomer and mathematician who first proposed a heliocentric model of the solar system, placing the sun instead of Earth at the center of the system and arranging the other planets in correct order from the sun. His argument for this bold theory hinged on his calculations of the relative sizes of the sun and Earth—he found the sun to be about 300 times larger—and a suspicion that the sun was really a star positioned close to Earth. Aristarchus was criticized by laypeople for impiety and by astronomers for proposing a theory that did not account for the observable retrograde motion of the planets—periods when planets seemed to switch direction and begin to move backward in the sky over the course of several weeks or months. Thus soundly trampled, Aristarchus's theory languished until Copernicus authored his revolutionary tract *Of the Revolutions of the Heavenly Spheres* in 1543. Although he briefly mentioned Aristarchus in an early draft, Copernicus decided to cross his name out of the book before publication.

Athanasius Kircher (1602–80) was a German Jesuit scholar and philosopher. Nicknamed "the master of a hundred arts" and sometimes called the last Renaissance man, Kircher taught mathematics, physics, and several languages at Collegio Romano, the first Jesuit university in the world. He also pioneered the study of Egyptian hieroglyphics and was the first to put forth the idea that the plague was caused by microorganisms. Kircher produced more than 40 weighty tomes on a bewildering variety of subjects, from China to musical theory to fossils to magnetism. In his spare time, Kircher terrorized the superstitious peasants of the countryside around his villa by sending up hot air balloons in the shape of dragons with the words "Flee the Wrath of God" blazoned on their bellies. He also constructed a great number of mechanical devices, such as speaking statues, megaphones, clocks, and musical instruments. The strangest by far was the cat piano: Caged cats with differently pitched voices were arranged side by side inside a conventional piano. When a piano key was depressed, a mechanism drove a spike into the appropriate cat's tail. "The result," wrote Kircher, "was a melody of meows that became more vigorous as the cats became more desperate. Who could not help but laugh at such music?" Who, indeed.

Eugène François Vidocq (1775–1857) was a French convict-turned-detective, reformer of the civil police force, and inventor of the criminal-fiction genre. After a misspent youth that left him wanted for manslaughter, forgery, robbery, and numerous prison escapes, Vidocq boldy presented himself to the prefect of police in Paris, offering his services as an insider to the criminal world in exchange for his freedom. Within a few years, Vidocq and several ex-convicts surpassed the police in the number of arrests made. This brigade de Surete ("security brigade") was the beginning of a civil police occupied with the active pursuit of criminals; before Vidocq's intervention, the activities of the police in large cities were mostly limited to political espionage and directing traffic. After resigning from the newly revolutionized police force, Vidocq published his memoirs, which were a big success and formed a lasting testimonial to Vidocq's character; today they are considered the first work of criminal fiction.

Nadezhda Andreyevna Durova (1783–1866) was a woman who joined the Russian army around the time of the Napoleonic wars. Reviled by her mother, who had wanted a boy, Durova was raised primarily by her father, a cavalry officer. Brash, fearless, and accustomed to horse-riding and sabre-swinging, Durova was in for a rude shock when her father gave her away in marriage at the age of 18 to a local court official. The marriage eventually ended, and Durova returned to her parents' house, leaving her ex-husband with an infant son. In 1807, she fled home dressed as a man and enlisted under a false name in a cavalry regiment. Several years later, she was discovered and brought before Czar Alexander I; Durova pleaded with him not to make her return to her intolerable life and begged to continue serving her country as a warrior. Moved by her plea, the czar gave her permission to remain in the army, decorated her with St. George's Cross for saving a fellow officer's life in battle, and raised her in rank. Durova retired in 1816 and wore masculine attire for the rest of her life. In her later years, she wrote of her army adventures in her widely read memoirs, *The Notes of a Cavalryman-Maiden*.

Ada Lovelace (1815–52) was the only legitimate daughter of the poet Lord Byron and the author of the first-ever computer program. Lord Byron and his wife, Annabella

Milbanke, had a tumultuous relationship. To prevent their daughter from following in his professional footsteps, Annabella gave her a rigorously mathematical education—rather unorthodox in the days when upper-class women were educated mostly in music, art, and languages. In her youth and adulthood, Ada was in close correspondence with mathematician Charles Babbage, who was highly impressed with her intellect. In 1841, Babbage gave a seminar at the University of Turin about the possibility of an "analytical engine": a mechanical calculating device capable of interpreting human instructions—in other words, a computer. After a young Italian engineer transcribed and published the lecture in French, Babbage asked Ada to translate it back into English and add her own notes to it. The notes took Ada about a year to complete and ultimately were more extensive than the paper itself; the last and longest of the seven sections describes an algorithm for the analytical engine to compute Bernoulli numbers. Because they contain the first set of instructions specifically intended for a computer, Ada Lovelace's notes are widely considered the world's first computer program, predating the first computer by about a century.

Sir Francis Galton (1822–1911) was a child prodigy and cousin of Charles Darwin. Among his accomplishments are extensive exploration of the African continent; the creation of the first weather map; coining the terms "eugenics" and "nature versus nurture"; the statistical concepts of correlation and regression to the mean; the first implementation of the survey as a method of data collection; Differential Psychology, also known as the London School of Experimental Psychology; the first scientific investigation into human fingerprints; and the biometric approach to genetics. On these and many other topics, Galton produced more than 340 papers and books throughout his lifetime. He received every major award the Victorian scientific community bestowed, and he was knighted in 1909.

William James Sidis (1898–1944) was possibly the smartest man who has ever lived. Sidis is believed to have had an IQ between 250 and 300. He was accepted to Harvard at the age of 11 after completing all of his primary and secondary schooling in seven months; he was also able to learn a new language a day and actually invented his own. However, constant media attention took its toll, and Sidis left the public eye soon after reaching adulthood, holding only menial jobs until his death from a stroke at the age of 46. The only topic to which he applied himself studiously and on which he produced a definitive text was streetcar transfers.

Norman Ernest Borlaug (1914–2009) was an American microbiologist and agricultural scientist who was instrumental in developing high-yield, disease-resistant wheat varieties in Latin America, Africa, and Asia. Borlaug effectively saved billions of people from starvation and was awarded the Nobel Peace Prize in 1970. According to the Congressional Tribute to Dr. Norman E. Borlaug Act of 2006, "Dr. Borlaug has saved more lives than any other person who has ever lived."

Vladimir Vysotsky (1938–80) was a Russian stage and film actor, writer, poet, and singer of immense talent and productivity. In the course of his relatively brief life, Vysotsky wrote between 600 and 800 songs about every aspect of Soviet living, from labor camps to popular TV shows. When not engaged in theater performances, concerts, or movie shoots, he wrote novels, novellas, short stories, and screenplays. Although the government refused to allow him to make records, fans defiantly taped his countless live concerts and distributed the recordings all over the country. Despite Vysotsky's ruthless satirizing of the poor living conditions in the U.S.S.R., he was all but immune from political prosecution by virtue of his stardom. Vysotsky died of heart failure in 1980, when the summer Olympics were in full swing in Moscow; to avoid rioting, the state-controlled media made no mention of the star's untimely demise. But the news quickly leaked out, and huge crowds began gathering at Taganka Theatre, where Vysotsky had played Hamlet until a week before his death. It's reported that close to a million people attended his funeral.

Charlemagne: Illiterate Reader

Charlemagne created a major Frankish Empire that unified most of what we now call western and central Europe, helped establish the dominance of the Roman Catholic Church in that area, began the Middle Ages, and brought about a revival of arts and literature that helped preserve the works of ancient Greek and Roman writers. Not bad for a fellow whose name isn't even known for certain!

The first mention of his name is the Latin *Carolus Magnus*, which translates as Charles the Great. The French, who claim him as one of their kings, call him Charlemagne (which translates more or less the same), while the Germans (who also claim him as their own) call him Karl der Grosse. The English-speaking world generally knows him by his French name, Charlemagne. We're not even entirely sure when he was born, though 742 is the commonly accepted date.

OF POPES AND KINGS

Charlemagne came from two lines of Frankish kings. His grandfather was the great Charles "The Hammer" Martel. Charles's tribe was known as the Merovingians, and Charles had largely unified modern-day France and had defeated the Arabian invaders at the Battle of Tours in 732. His son, Pepin the Short, was eventually made king and established a new line known as the Carolingians. The pope stated his approval for this, starting a tradition of kings seeking the pope's approval, a situation that often led to religious wars and other difficulties. When Pepin died, his two sons, Charles and Carloman, ruled together until Carloman died in 771, leaving Charles to rule the kingdom. Charles went on to gain historic renown.

Like so many great people in history, Charlemagne earned much of his reputation through military conquest. Over the years, he fought in Italy, Saxony, Spain, Bavaria, and pretty much anywhere else he was threatened. His campaign in Spain was immortalized by the epic poem "Song of Roland." A devout Christian, Charlemagne went to the aid of the pope several times. On Christmas Day 800, Pope Leo III crowned Charlemagne holy roman emperor. There is some dispute as to whether or not Charlemagne was really aware that this was going to happen, but he is said to have remarked later that allowing it to happen had been a mistake. Kings and emperors wanted to rule as the top dog, and having a pope approve or—worse yet—actually crown you as king meant that even in temporal matters the pope was above the emperor. It wasn't until Napoleon crowned himself in 1804 that this conflict was finally resolved in favor of the power of the state.

SAVIOR OF WESTERN CIVILIZATION

One might think, given all this fighting, that Charlemagne didn't have much time for anything else. To the contrary, Charlemagne's biggest contributions to history may well be what he did off the battlefield. Here are just a few of the major cultural contributions made by Charlemagne:

◈ After the fall of the Roman Empire, education in Europe had gone into a steep decline. Charlemagne reversed that trend by increasing the number of schools. His palace school in the capital of Aachen featured Alcuin of York, perhaps the top scholar of his day. The school, and the nearby court, were crowded with other leading minds of that age, and Charlemagne and his sons attended classes from time to time. Not bad for a fellow who couldn't write. On the other hand, he could read, and most kings in those days were completely illiterate. Oh yes, one thing more: Education was normally reserved for the nobility, but Charlemagne made sure that really deserving commoners also had a chance to be educated. He understood that the more educated people there were, the more people there would be to help run things. Charlemagne also encouraged the education of women and established empire-wide curriculum standards.

◈ The script of the period was difficult to read. Scholars and scribes under Charlemagne eventually came up with a new system that used both upper and lowercase letters. This script is called Carolingian Minuscule and is one of the foundations of modern Western script.

◈ The works of the ancients were in danger of being lost. Many ancient documents had been destroyed by Christian clergy who were determined that people should only have Christian materials to read. Since they were all handwritten, there were obviously not many copies available. So, when one was lost, that was likely all she wrote (so to speak). Charlemagne established writing centers where scribes spent all day making copies of these works. He sent other people all over the countryside, peeking into musty old monastic libraries, trying to find copies of ancient texts that could then be copied. Many, if not most, of the ancient works that we still have were saved due to this effort.

◈ Given all of this, it may not surprise you to hear that Charlemagne was a great fan of books. He would give and receive books, often bound in sumptuous ivory and jewels. Those that survive today are wonders to behold.

These educational and literary accomplishments, along with some other reforms, have led historians to give Charlemagne credit for starting the Carolingian Renaissance, or a rebirth of learning and of interest in the ancient texts. Some historians even feel that he was largely responsible for saving Western civilization. When he died in 814, his empire began a decline, and within a generation had broken into a feudal system that would last through much of the Middle Ages. Emphasis on learning and literature would decline as well, but thanks to Charlemagne, it never completely died out. When the Italian Renaissance began several centuries later, scholars had a base upon which to begin their march to the modern era; a base that was created by Charlemagne, one of history's greatest figures.

A Few Who Saved Many

During World War II, many individuals worked to save Jews from extermination by the Nazis, risking their own freedom or lives in the process. Here are four individuals whose courage and moral fortitude saved thousands.

RAOUL WALLENBERG

Wallenberg was a Swedish diplomat stationed in Budapest who saved more than 100,000 Hungarian Jews from July to December 1944. He designed, issued, and personally distributed some 4,500 "protective passports" that gave Jewish holders perceived safe passage to Sweden under the protection of the Swedish Crown. Wallenberg issued at least another 12,000 passports. When acting personally, he often handed the passports to Jews aboard trains awaiting deportation and convinced authorities they were to be released under his protection. He also established havens for Jews in Budapest homes, dubbed "Swedish houses" because they flew the Swedish flag and were declared Swedish territory. Finally, he used diplomatic and moral pressure to prevent the liquidation of the Jewish ghettos in Budapest. On January 17, 1945, Wallenberg was arrested by Soviet agents and never seen again. In 2000, the Russians admitted his wrongful imprisonment and reported that he died in captivity in 1947, a claim that many still doubt.

YVONNE NÈVEJEAN

Nèvejean headed the Oeuvre Nationale de l'Enfance (ONE), a Belgian agency supervising children's homes. Funded by underground Jewish organizations and the Belgian government-in-exile, Nèvejean rescued more than 4,000 Jewish children by providing them with new identities, ration cards, and places of permanent refuge in private homes and institutions. She also arranged for the release of a group of children taken by the Gestapo to an internment camp to be readied for deportation. Children rescued by Nèvejean became known as "Yvonne's children."

SUGIHARA (SEMPO) CHIUNE

Sugihara was the Japanese consul general in Kovno at the time of the Soviet invasion of Lithuania. When the Soviets ordered all foreign delegations out of Kovno in July 1940, Sugihara asked for a 20-day extension and, in defiance of explicit orders from the Japanese Foreign Ministry, issued transit visas to Polish and Lithuanian Jews seeking to escape both the Nazis and the Soviets. Through August 1940, he and his wife, Yukiko, worked day and night signing papers for Jews waiting in long lines around the Japanese consulate building. In a race against time, he provided lifesaving documents for more than 6,000 "Sugihara Survivors," signing papers and shoving them through the train window even as he was leaving Kovno. "I should follow my conscience," he said at the time. "I cannot allow these people to die, people who had come to me for help with death staring them in the eyes."

OSKAR SCHINDLER

Immortalized in the film *Schindler's List*, Schindler was a German businessman and Nazi Party member who entertained and bribed German Army and SS officials in Poland to obtain contracts and Jewish labor for an enamel kitchenware factory in Krakow he had taken over from a Jewish firm. Awakened to the fact by his Jewish accountant that work in his factory meant survival for Jews, Schindler hired more Jews than he needed, convincing SS officials with bribes that he needed their "essential" skills. In all, he saved more than 1,300 "Schindlerju-den" by employing them in his various factories. When Nazis who elected to ignore Schindler's "arrangement" put scores of Schindler workers onto a train headed for Auschwitz, Oskar came up with additional bribes, and had the workers released into his custody. "If you saw a dog going to be crushed under a car," he said later of his actions, "wouldn't you help him?"

Dorie Miller: An Unlikely Hero

Doris "Dorie" Miller, so named because his mom's midwife had expected a girl, stood that early December 1941 morning on the deck of the USS *West Virginia*. Trained as a cook, no one would have thought he'd emerge from Pearl Harbor as a hero.

DECEMBER 7, 1941

Twenty-year-old "Dorie" Miller joined the navy in September 1939. He enrolled at the recruiting post in his hometown of Waco, Texas, after taking a ride in the back of the bus with a group of other black recruits. Blacks in the navy were then restricted to kitchen duty. So when he enrolled, Miller became a mess attendant, eventually working his way up to ship's cook.

On an otherwise sleepy Sunday, Miller watched as an array of aircraft drew near. Two sections of the squadron dove toward the harbor and the airfield at adjacent Ford Island. Alongside his ship, the *West Virginia*, was the battleship *Tennessee*. Along the quays forward were the *Maryland* and the *Oklahoma*, and to the stern was the *Arizona*. Unlike most of the crew, Miller was on duty that morning, collecting officers' laundry. Although barred from a combat post because of his race, he had proved himself a fighter—he was the *West Virginia*'s heavy-weight boxing champ.

It was odd, Miller thought, that aircraft were training so close to a naval and air base. Then four of the planes dove *toward* Ford Island. Suddenly, the airport's hangar and a clutch of Devastor dive-bombers on the runways exploded. Miller later recalled, "I found myself an unwilling occupant of a front-row seat from which to witness the proceedings."

Miller watched another group of planes, rising suns on their wings, veer down toward the *West Virginia*, and drop five 18-inch-wide torpedoes into the waves. Within seconds, the ship shuddered and heaved from massive explosions. Soon after, Japanese planes dropped two armor-piercing bombs into the battleship, sparking massive fires.

The ship's communications officer pressed Miller into action—the captain was bleeding badly and had to be moved. Miller and the officer made a nightmarish journey through the dark, smoke-filled corridors of the vessel. En route, Miller felt a gigantic explosion—not from the *West Virginia*, as it turned out, but from the nearby USS *Arizona*, which had blown up, taking the lives of 1,177 men. Employing his strength as a boxer and an ex-high-school fullback, Miller helped hoist the gravely injured captain to the forecastle, and later to the bridge.

Back on deck, Miller saw the ship was listing; water poured over the side. Just ahead, Miller could see the now-capsized hull of the *Oklahoma*. He pulled wounded sailors on the main deck to the relative safety of the quarterdeck. Miller and Lieutenant Commander Frederic White then turned to a half-dozen survivors bobbing in the fiery, oily waters alongside their battleship. He and White tossed out ropes, hauled the sailors aboard, and then collapsed from exhaustion. However, the force of 181 Japanese aircraft continued their bombing and strafing runs.

Miller and White rushed to a pair of Browning .50-caliber antiaircraft machine guns. Even as a cook, Miller had been trained for combat, but not specifically in the use of antiaircraft guns. He put his training in gear. "The sky seemed filled with diving planes and the black bursts of exploding antiaircraft shells," he remembered. He tracked a swooping Japanese plane through the gun sight, his thumbs squeezing the firing levers. Smoke billowed out of the aircraft. Seconds later, it crashed, throwing up a great plume of water from the embattled harbor.

"It wasn't hard," Miller stated. "I just pulled the trigger and she worked fine. I had watched the others with these guns. I guess I fired her for about 15 minutes." As the attackers tried to finish off the U.S. Pacific Fleet, Miller and a few other gunners battled back. Finally, the *West Virginia* settled into the shallow harbor, with 130 of its 1,541-man crew killed. Miller and other survivors swung over by rope to the waiting *Tennessee*.

STATESIDE RECOGNITION

Word spread back to the mainland about Miller's Pearl Harbor heroism. The *Pittsburgh Courier*, a prominent black newspaper, campaigned to have the sailor decorated. And in May 1942, Admiral Chester W. Nimitz, commander of the Pacific Fleet, stood on the aircraft carrier USS *Enterprise* and personally awarded Miller the Navy Cross, the service's third-highest decoration. Said Nimitz: "This marks the first time in this conflict that such high tribute has been made in the Pacific Fleet to a member of his race and I'm sure that the future will see others similarly honored for brave acts." Capitalizing on Miller's fame, the navy sent him stateside on a war-bonds tour, with stops in his hometown of Waco, in Dallas, and at Chicago's Great Lakes Naval Training Center, which had begun training blacks for positions more responsible than mess attendant.

DORIE RETURNS TO SERVICE

One more war mission awaited Miller. He was onboard the escort carrier USS *Liscome Bay*, whose planes supported the bloody but successful November 1943 invasion of Tarawa atoll. As the invasion fleet was readying to leave the area, the Japanese submarine I-175 struck the carrier. Its torpedo ignited the magazine and practically tore off the vessel's stern where Miller was manning an antiaircraft gun. He was most likely killed instantly (though not officially presumed dead until a year and a day later). Three hundred seventy-three of his fellow 646 crewmen were also killed.

Miller's courage against the enemy and against the racial codes of the day had great effect. In February 1944, the navy commissioned its first black officers, and in 1948, President Truman formally integrated all branches of the U.S. armed services. A final legacy of Miller's was the commissioning in 1973 of the Knox-class frigate the USS *Miller*, which saw service in the Persian Gulf, Black Sea, and elsewhere.

Orator, Author, Abolitionist—and Slave

One of the most influential American writers and lecturers of the 19th century was a man who was not sure what day he had been born and had to change his name to keep from being returned to slavery.

Frederick Bailey, who later became internationally renowned as Frederick Douglass, was born the son of a black slave mother and an unknown white father in Maryland. Although he once thought his date of birth lay somewhere in February 1818, he was never certain of the year, and his calculations later in life led him to believe he had been born in 1816. Douglass grew up surrounded by the brutality of slavery.

ESCAPE FROM SHACKLES

Trained as a shipwright (and having secretly learned how to read), young Frederick Bailey made a daring escape to freedom in 1838 and eventually ended up in Massachusetts. He took the name Douglass to reduce his chances of being identified as an escaped slave. Soon after, he met abolitionist William Lloyd Garrison, who hired him to lecture for his Anti-Slavery Society. Like his new friend and mentor, Douglass attacked the institution of slavery in the most vehement terms: "I assert most unhesitatingly that the religion of the South is a mere covering for the most horrid crimes—a justifier of the most appalling barbarity, a sanctifier of the most hateful frauds, and a dark shelter under which the darkest, foulest, grossest, and most infernal deeds of slaveholders find the strongest protection."

ACHIEVING SUCCESS

Douglass achieved national prominence with the 1845 publication of his first book, *Narrative of the Life of Frederick Douglass, an American Slave*. Immediately fearing arrest and re-enslavement, he went to Great Britain for two years, traveling throughout England, Ireland, and Scotland. He gave human rights lectures in many locales (mostly Protestant churches) and became a very popular figure. Befriending Irish Nationalist Daniel O'Connell and feeling treated not "as a color, but as a man," these were important years for Douglass. As a testament to his influence in the British Isles, there remains to this day a colorful mural dedicated to him in Belfast. During the time he was in Britain, friends purchased his freedom from his Maryland owner, and he was able to return triumphantly to New England. Soon after, Douglass launched the abolitionist newspaper *North Star*, which in 1851 merged with the *Liberty Party Paper* and officially became *Frederick Douglass's Paper*.

BECOMING A MAN OF INFLUENCE

As might be expected, the fiery Douglass exerted some of his greatest influence on the struggle against slavery during the war, urging abolition no longer simply on moral grounds but as a means of taking a critical strategic asset from the rebellious South. He also campaigned for the federal government to allow blacks to serve as soldiers. In both of these efforts, he was ultimately successful.

President Lincoln respected Douglass's opinions on emancipation, and the two conferred on a number of occasions. Douglass repeatedly urged the President to proclaim that the emancipation of slaves was the supreme purpose of the war, but Lincoln was frank in explaining that he couldn't do that until it would actually benefit the war effort. Looking for an opportunity, he finally found one after a Confederate advance into the North was stopped at Antietam, and Lincoln announced the Emancipation Proclamation. That new policy went into effect on New Year's Day 1863, to tremendous celebration by Douglass and other abolitionists.

BRINGING BLACK TROOPS TO THE FIGHT

As a great orator and respected member of the black community, Douglass also recruited regiments of U.S. Colored Troops. "Fly to arms," he urged, "and smite with death the power that would bury the government and your liberty in the same hopeless grave." These regiments included the famous 54th Massachusetts, in which two of his sons served, and the 55th Massachusetts. Douglass was disappointed however, with how poorly these units were treated and with the fact that they were paid less than their white counterparts, so he continued to work tirelessly on their behalf.

PUBLIC SERVICE

After the war, Douglass did not cease his activism but in fact added the duties of a public official. Throughout the years, he served as U.S. marshal to the District of Columbia, recorder of deeds for the District of Columbia, U.S. minister to Haiti, and chargé d'affaires to Saint Domingue. He published several more books and essays.

Douglass's first wife, Anna Douglass, died in 1882, and Douglass married Helen Pitts in 1884. Pitts was a white feminist 20 years his junior, which caused quite the scandal at the time. Douglass also began aligning himself with feminist causes and spent his later days traveling extensively throughout Europe. He finally retired to his home in Washington, D.C., where he died at age 77—or 79, depending on how you count it.

Emiliano Zapata

Most people know Emiliano Zapata as the revolutionary leader of southern Mexico who, along with Poncho Villa in the North, fought in the Mexican Revolution. Some also know him as the subject of the film *Viva Zapata!*, starring Marlon Brando, for which John Steinbeck wrote a masterful screenplay. Few, however, know him as the spiritual and intellectual father of Mexico's land reform movement. But Emiliano Zapata, who loved nothing more than the lifestyle of the agrarian village in which he was raised, was a passionate proponent of land-use rights for Mexican farmers.

LAND AND LIBERTY

At the start of the 20th century, Mexico's small farmers were becoming increasingly disenfranchised by the powerful *hacienda* owners who sought to supplant the native corn crop with the more internationally valuable sugarcane plant. Through intimidation, violence, and indentured servitude, the *hacienda* owners—and the government that backed them—steadily encroached upon land that had been farmed by peasant families for generations.

In 1909, the village of Anenecuilco, in the small central-Mexico state of Morelos, elected Emiliano Zapata to the traditional post of defender of the village's interests. The orphaned son of a prosperous but humble local mestizo family whose ancestors had fought against the Spanish and the French, Zapata was a perfect fit for the position. He worked to establish land rights for farmers through ancient title deeds and petitioned the government to recognize the farmers' rightful ownership of their lands. Sometimes he was able to settle land disputes through diplomacy, but the lack of government support increasingly frustrated him.

In 1910, just a year after Zapata's election, the Mexican Revolution began. Zapata, who counseled the villagers to farm with rifles over their shoulders, joined the forces of

Francisco Madero, a revolutionary who planned to overthrow Mexican President Porfirio Díaz. Zapata became a general of the Liberation Army of the South and aided Madero to success. Díaz was overthrown, and Francisco Madero became the new president of Mexico. Unfortunately, Zapata was soon disappointed by the slow pace of land reform under Madero, and relations between the two former allies broke down.

By this time, Zapata had become a popular leader. His soft-spoken but passionate dedication to the peasants' cause attracted thousands of people willing to fight for the right to farm their own land as they pleased. Through a succession of corrupt leaders and broken promises, Zapata maintained his agrarian ideals and his rallying slogan of *Tierra y Libertad* (Land and Liberty).

THE "LIBERAL-BOURGEOIS" REVOLUTIONARY

Zapata's ideology found its fruition in the Plan de Ayala, a radical document that outlined a plan for land reform that Zapata wrote with his former teacher and mentor, Otilio Montaño Sanchez, in 1911. Though awkwardly worded, full of misspellings, and rife with redundancies, the land reform proposed by the Plan de Ayala was incendiary and galvanized support around Zapata's movement. Though Zapata admired Communist ideas, he considered Marxism impractical and instead simply sought to return the land to those from whom it had been taken.

When the Plan de Ayala was first printed, the intellectual elite in Mexico City scoffed at the poorly written work. Zapata's old enemy, President Francisco Madero, gave the editor of the *Diario del Hogar* permission to reprint the Plan de Ayala, reportedly saying, "Publish it so that everybody will know how crazy Zapata is." The plan backfired, and the Plan de Ayala received enthusiastic support that eventually led to Madero's ousting.

In the Plan de Ayala, Zapata did not seek to destroy the *hacienda* system, but rather to place legal checks upon its powers to seize and hold land. Under the Plan de Ayala, *ejidas*, or communally held lands, would be re-established in the villages that chose such a system. Alternately, the farmers could elect to establish individual plots. Zapata's ideology has since been labeled "liberal-bourgeois" or "bourgeois democratic," as it was truly an inclusionary, practical system that maintained as its primary goal peasant enfranchisement without recourse to completely subverting the existing capitalistic system.

LIFE AFTER DEATH

The corrupt revolutionary leader Venustiano Carranza (who took over the reins of power from President Madero) consolidated his power by ordering his followers to assassinate Zapata in 1919. After Zapata was killed, the government forces took pictures of his face while shining a flashlight upon it to prove he was dead.

The agrarian leader's ideas were not so easily dispatched, however. Soon after Zapata's murder, men who had been sympathetic to Zapata's philosophy ousted Carranza and began to institute the land reform policies championed by their fallen leader. Today's Zapatistas, the spiritual descendants of Emiliano, have departed markedly from the specifics of the Plan de Ayala, but they retain the goal of uplifting the peasant class by striving against social injustice and government interference.

CHAPTER 6

NOTABLE GROUPS

The Druids and the Picts

What do you know about the Druids? How about the Picts? Chances are, what you know (or think you know) is wrong.

Most contemporary perceptions of the Druids and Picts are derived from legend and lore. As such, our conceptions of these peoples range from erroneous and unlikely to just plain foolish.

Let's start with the Druids. They are often credited with the building of Stonehenge, the great stone megalith believed to be their sacred temple as well as their arena for savage human sacrifice rituals. True or False?

False. First of all, Stonehenge was built around 2000 B.C.—1,400 years before the Druids emerged. Second, though we know admittedly little of Druidic practice, it seemed to be traditional and conservative. It is not known whether the Druids actually carried out human sacrifices.

What about the Picts? Although often reduced to a mythical race of magical fairies, the Picts actually ruled Scotland before the Scots.

So who were the Druids and the Picts?

THE DRUIDS—THE PRIESTLY CLASS

As the priestly class of Celtic society, the Druids were the Celts' spiritual leaders—repositories of knowledge about the world and the universe, as well as authorities on Celtic history, law, and religion. They were the preservers of Celtic culture.

The Druids preached of the power and authority of the deities and taught the immortality of the soul and reincarnation. They had an innate connection to all things living and preferred holding great rituals among natural shrines—the forests, springs, and groves.

To become a Druid, one had to devote as many as 20 years to study and preparation.

MORE POWERFUL THAN CELTIC CHIEFTAINS

In terms of power, the Druids took a backseat to no one. Even the Celtic chieftains, well-versed in power politics, recognized the overarching authority of the Druids. Celtic society had well-defined power and social structures and territories and property rights. The Druids were deemed the ultimate arbiters in all matters relating to such. If there was a legal or financial dispute between two parties, it was unequivocally settled in special Druid-presided courts. Armed conflicts were immediately ended by Druid rulings. Their word was final.

In the end, however, there were two forces to which even the Druids had to succumb—the Romans and Christianity. With the Roman invasion of Britain in

A.D. 43, Emperor Claudius decreed that Druidism was to be outlawed throughout the Roman Empire. The Romans destroyed the last vestiges of official Druidism in Britain with the annihilation of the Druid stronghold of Anglesey in A.D. 61. Surviving Druids fled to unconquered Ireland and Scotland, only to become completely marginalized within a few centuries.

Stripped of power and status, the Druids of ancient Celtic society disappeared. They morphed into wandering poets and storytellers with no connection to their once illustrious past.

THE PICTS—THE PAINTED PEOPLE

The Picts were, in simplest terms, the people who inhabited ancient Scotland before the Scots. Their origins are unknown, but some scholars believe that the Picts were descendants of the Caledonians or other Iron Age tribes who invaded Britain.

No one knows what the Picts called themselves; the origin of their name comes from other sources and probably derives from the Pictish custom of tattooing or painting their bodies. The Irish called them *Cruithni*, meaning "the people of the designs." The Romans called them *Picti*, which is Latin for "painted people"; however, the Romans probably used the term as a general moniker for all the untamed peoples living north of Hadrian's Wall.

A SECONDHAND HISTORY

The Picts themselves left no written records. All descriptions of their history and culture come from secondhand accounts. The earliest of these is a Roman account from A.D. 297 stating that the Picti and the Hiberni (Irish) were already well-established enemies of the Britons to the south.

The Picts were also well-established enemies of each other. Before the arrival of the Romans, the Picts spent most of their time fighting amongst themselves. The threat posed by the Roman conquest of Britain forced the squabbling Pict kingdoms to come together and eventually evolve into the nation-state of Pictland. The united Picts were strong enough not only to resist conquest by the Romans, but also to launch periodic raids on Roman-occupied Britain.

Having defied the Romans, the Picts later succumbed to a more benevolent invasion launched by Irish Christian missionaries. Arriving in Pictland in the late 6th century, they succeeded in converting the polytheistic Pict elite within two decades. Much of the written history of the Picts comes from the Irish Christian annals. If not for the writings of the Romans and the Irish missionaries, we might not have knowledge of the Picts at all.

Despite the existence of an established Pict state, Pictland disappeared with the changing of its name to the Kingdom of Alba in A.D. 843, a move signifying the rise of the Gaels as the dominant people in Scotland. By the 11th century, virtually all vestiges of the Picts had vanished.

The Rise and Fall of the Knights Templar

The Crusades, Christendom's quest to recover and hold the Holy Land, saw the rise of several influential military orders. Of these, the Knights Templar had perhaps the greatest lasting influence—and took the hardest fall.

July 15, 1099: On that day, the First Crusade stormed Jerusalem and slaughtered everyone in sight—Jews, Muslims, Christians—it didn't matter. This unleashed a wave of pilgrimage, as European Christians flocked to now-accessible Palestine and its holy sites. Though Jerusalem's loss was a blow to Islam, it was a bonanza for the region's thieves, as it brought a steady stream of naive pilgrims to rob.

DEFENDING THE FAITHFUL

French knight Hugues de Payen, with eight chivalrous comrades, swore to guard the travelers. In 1119, they gathered at the Church of the Holy Sepulchre and pledged their lives to poverty, chastity, and obedience before King Baldwin II of Jerusalem. The Order of Poor Knights of the Temple of Solomon took up headquarters in said Temple.

GOING MAINSTREAM

The Templars did their work well, and in 1127 Baldwin sent a Templar embassy to Europe to secure a marriage that would ensure the royal succession in Jerusalem. Not only did they succeed, they became rock stars of sorts. Influential nobles showered the Order with money and real estate, the foundation of its future wealth. With this growth came a formal code of rules. Some highlights include:

◈ Templars could not desert the battlefield or leave a castle by stealth.

◈ They had to wear white habits—except for sergeants and squires, who could wear black.

◈ They had to tonsure (shave) their crowns and wear beards.

◈ They were required to dine in communal silence, broken only by Scriptural readings.

◈ Templars had to be chaste, except for married men joining with their wives' consent.

A LAW UNTO THEMSELVES

Now with offices in Europe to manage the Order's growing assets, the Templars returned to Palestine to join in the Kingdom's ongoing defense. In 1139, Pope Innocent II decreed the Order answerable only to the Holy See. Now the Order was entitled to accept tithes! The Knights Templar had come far.

By the mid-1100s, the Templars had become a church within a church, a nation within a nation, and a major banking concern. Templar keeps were well-defended depositories, and the Order became financiers to the crowned heads of Europe—even to the Papacy. Their reputation for meticulous bookkeeping and secure transactions underpinned Europe's financial markets, even as their soldiers kept fighting for the faith in the Holy Land.

DOWNFALL

The Crusaders couldn't hold the Holy Land. In 1187, Saladin the Kurd retook Jerusalem, martyring 230 captured Templars. Factional fighting between Christians sped the collapse. In 1291, the last Crusader outpost fell to the Mamelukes of Egypt. The Templars' troubles had just begun.

King Philip IV of France owed the Order a lot of money, and in 1307, Philip ordered all Templars arrested. They stood accused of devil worship, sodomy, and greed. Hideous torture produced piles of confessions. The Order was looted and officially dissolved. In March 1314, Jacques de Molay, the last Grand Master of the Knights Templar, was burned at the stake.

Many Templar assets passed to the Knights Hospitallers. The Order survived in Portugal as the Order of Christ, where it exists to this day in form similar to British knightly orders. A Templar fleet escaped from La Rochelle and vanished; it may have reached Scotland. Swiss folktales suggest that some Templars took their loot and expertise to Switzerland, possibly laying the groundwork for what would one day become the Swiss banking industry.

The Bavarian Illuminati

Before delving into the intricacies of the Illuminati's origin, we'd recommend donning a tinfoil hat. It will protect you against the New World Order conspiracy.

What does *Illuminati* actually mean?
"The Enlightened." Like many religious faiths and secret societies, the original Bavarian Illuminati were founded in search of enlightenment. Prior groups with similar ideas used similar names.

Did earlier Illuminati groups evolve into the Bavarian Illuminati?
Well, let's examine some earlier groups. Spain's *Alumbrados* ("enlightened") dated to the time of Columbus (1490s), suffered from the Inquisition, and developed a following in France (as the *Illuminés*) that endured until the late 1700s, when the French Revolution sat on them. The *Rosicrucians* started in Germany in the early 1600s, claiming lineage from the Knights Templar; by the late 1770s, their theme was becoming increasingly Egyptian. Many Rosicrucians were also Freemasons, a group with unbroken lineage to the present day.

They all had ideas in common with the Bavarian Illuminati; however, the Bavarian Illuminati sprang from the fertile mind of an iconoclastic law professor, not from a previous group. At most, the Bavarian group experienced some cross-pollination with other similar groups (notably Freemasonry), but that doesn't equal ancestral continuity.

How'd the Bavarian group get going?

It began in Ingolstadt, Bavaria, with a German 20-something named Adam Weishaupt. In 1775, Weishaupt accepted a natural and canon law professorship at the University of Ingolstadt that had recently been vacated by an ejected Jesuit.

Weishaupt was a maverick prone to anticlerical utterances: the anti-Jesuit, if you will. He soon managed to convince himself, without irony, that he was destined to lead humanity out of superstition toward enlightenment. Unsurprisingly, the Jesuits hated his guts.

Evidently, Weishaupt couldn't afford the Masons' fees, so he launched the Perfectibilists (later the Bavarian Illuminati) on May 1, 1776 (this would later fuel plentiful conspiracy theories about May Day celebrations). Fascinated with Egyptian stuff, he assigned his society a pyramid as its symbol.

Did this group extend tentacles into business, government, and church?

To extend tentacles, one must first possess some. The Illuminati concerned themselves mostly with secret degrees and titles, plus absolute obedience to the chain of command with Weishaupt at the top. There is no evidence the group ever controlled anything. Illuminati were supposed to spurn superstition and strive toward rationalism to help perfect each other's mentalities. The meta-goal was clearing the earth of inhumanity and stupidity. It actually sounds more than a little like modern Scientology, at least in terms of stated goals (as opposed to reality).

That sounds like the vision of a new world order.
It is. The modern conspiracy question rests not in the nature of the original Bavarian Illuminati, which is well documented, but rather to what degree it has survived to exert control over modern affairs. As any nightly news broadcast will show, their work didn't make a lasting dent in either inhumanity or stupidity.

Why not?
Could it be because inhumanity and stupidity are so very human? Think of the Illuminati as a die intended to mint enlightened persons. This die possessed one fundamental crack: Its concept of enlightenment categorically discouraged questioning the autocratic leader. That's no way to run a freethinkers' group. In such groups, true freethinkers drift away, leaving only quasi-freethinkers who don't argue with the Maximum Leader.

But the organization still grew. Why?
It only grew for a brief time, and that had much to do with the work of Baron Adolph Knigge, who joined in the 1780s. Knigge was both well-known and a capable administrator who gave the Illuminati a great deal of practical Masonic wisdom, helping sort out Weishaupt's rather rinky-dink organization. By its peak in 1784, it had several thousand members.

What sent it downhill?
First there was the inevitable squabble between Weishaupt and Knigge, which ended with Knigge telling Weishaupt where to shove his little fiefdom. It's tempting to blame the whole thing on Weishaupt, but the evidence indicates that Knigge had an ego to match Weishaupt's and could be just as great a horse's posterior. The death-blow came when Duke Karl Theodor of Bavaria banned all unauthorized secret societies.

Did that simply shatter the organism into many pieces that grew independently?

Evidence suggests that the ban, plus police raids, shattered the Illuminati into dying pieces rather than living ones. Sacked from teaching, Weishaupt fled to a neighboring state and died in obscurity.

Others tried to keep Illuminati islets alive, without evident success. Like witchcraft of an earlier age, the actual practice became far rarer than the accusation—and official paranoia over secret societies and sedition kept the term *Illuminati* cropping up.

So, why does the intrigue linger?

Perhaps for the same reason the Freemasons, Knights Templar, and so forth keep showing up in conspiracy theories: When someone wants to point to a potential conspiracy, he or she can usually find some bit of circumstantial evidence hinting a connection to one of the above. Those who disagree, of course, must be toadies of the conspiracy! It's an argument that can't end.

But insofar as we are guided by actual evidence, the Bavarian Illuminati did end. Whatever world conspiracies there might be today, it's doubtful any descend directly from Weishaupt's ideological treehouse club.

Lords of the Rising Sun

For nearly 800 years, they held the power of life and death in the Heavenly Kingdom. The supreme lords of the samurai, they were called *shogun*.

THE RISE OF THE SHOGUN

Since ancient times, the title *sei-i taishogun*, or "great general who subdues barbarians," had been awarded to the highest military officers recognized by Japan's imperial court at Kyoto. But in A.D. 1184, the title took on a new, more powerful meaning. That year, General Minamoto Yoritomo wrested power from the emperor during a brutal civil war. Thus was born the *shogunate*, a period in which the emperor retained formal power—as mandated by heaven—but where the real power lay with the shogun (the short form of *sei-i taishogun*) and his administrators.

Two great houses nominally ruled a patchwork of warring feudal provinces from 1192 to 1600, when one climactic battle settled Japan's affairs for the next two and a half centuries. At the Battle of Sekigahara, nearly 150,000 samurai, retainers, musketeers, and men-at-arms viciously fought against one another in two rival factions. General Tokugawa Ieyasu destroyed his rivals and emerged as master of Japan.

Tokugawa established the Tokugawa shogunate at Edo (now called Tokyo) and began his reign by redistributing lands and political power among his most loyal vassals. Two years after taking office, he abdicated, putting into practice the Japanese custom of officially retiring but sharing the governing of the country with his son, Hidetada. Hidetada and his successors consolidated the shogun's authority, and the Tokugawa dynasty survived as the dominant Japanese government until 1868.

RULE BY THE SWORD

The Tokugawa ruled Japan with an iron fist. Its early governors banned Christianity and other Western influences. They established a formal caste system that placed *samurai*, the warrior class akin to Western knights, at the top of the hierarchy, followed by farmers, artisans, and merchants. The great *han*, or provinces (akin to European duchies), were ruled by the *daimyo*, powerful nobles who were required to live at the Edo court every other year and keep their family members in Edo when they spent their alternating years at home.

In the late 1630s to early 1640s, the Tokugawa imposed sharp limitations on foreign business and immigration that created an insular kingdom little known to the outside world until the turbulent 19th century. As a result of this strict control, Japan grew up in isolation, creating new forms of philosophy, poetry, and literature within its borders and promoting trade almost exclusively within the kingdom.

The shogunate system was efficient but inflexible and fostered a groundswell of local dissent that percolated under the surface during its 264-year reign. Lower classes chafed at the impossibility of advancement, while the business class became frustrated by the shogun's monopoly on foreign trade.

BREAKING THE SWORD

In the mid-1800s, foreign powers pushed Japan into accepting the outside world. In 1853, Commodore Matthew Perry led a U.S. naval squadron into Tokyo Bay in a dramatic display of American military might, and the following year coerced the shogun into opening diplomatic relations with the United States. As foreign powers forced the shogunate to open its borders, Japanese liberals began pressing for a restoration of the emperor's powers. The last Tokugawa shogun abdicated his throne in November 1867, and civil war broke out between forces backing Emperor Meiji and those of the former shogun. The Boshin War, or "War of the Year of the Dragon," ended in early 1869 with the destruction of the emperor's foes, many of whom met their ends in the ancient suicide ritual of *seppuku*.

The age of the mighty shogun had ended.

Peace Churches

The Protestant Reformation of the 1500s sent Christians flying in all directions. The Anabaptists (Mennonites, Amish, Brethren, and Hutterites) and Friends (Quakers) represented some of the more radical trends in late medieval Christian thought.

ANABAPTISTS

The word *Anabaptist* means "rebaptizer." In early 1525, a group of young Swiss Christians agreed that Christian faith should be an informed adult decision, not something imposed upon an infant. Anabaptists baptized one another and planned to put off baptizing their children until they were of age.

Anabaptism spread swiftly throughout German-speaking Europe and the Netherlands. Many of its adherents paid the ultimate price for their "heresy," however. Amid gruesome persecution and martyrdom, they began to scatter, forming the sects described as follows.

MENNONITES

Father Menno Simons, a Dutch Catholic priest, became an Anabaptist in 1536. Soon, his followers began to call themselves Mennonites, and most eventually moved to Prussia and Russia. In the 1870s, they joined the great waves of immigration to the United States. Today, there are some 350,000 Mennonites in the United States. They range from communal groups (who practice with varying degrees of strictness) to mainstream urban dwellers who simply attend Mennonite services.

AMISH

By 1693, some Mennonites in Alsace (modern France) felt the movement had lost its way. Under the leadership of Jakob Ammann, they separated to form their own communities removed from worldly influence and corruption. During the following century, Amish groups started migrating to the Americas. Nearly all of today's approximately 330,000 Amish live in the United States. Their strict communities are the most conservative of all Anabaptist groups.

BRETHREN

The story of the German Baptist Brethren begins (not surprisingly) in Germany in 1708 with Alexander Mack. Mack's congregants embraced many Anabaptist beliefs and found themselves mockingly called "Dunkers" by the general public for their practice of baptism by immersion. By 1740, nearly all had moved to what would soon become the United States. Today, there are some 215,000 North American Brethren, mostly in the United States. Some Brethren subgroups are very conservative, others less so.

HUTTERITES

In 1528, one group of Anabaptists fled to Moravia, taking their name from leader Jakob Hutter. Their efforts to live in communal peace came to naught in Moravia; Hutter himself was burned alive in 1535.

In 1770, the small Hutterite remnant fled to Russia. One hundred years after that, the group began a migration to Canada. Today, they number approximately 24,000. About 70 percent live in Canada's western provinces, pursuing a communal farming lifestyle. Dedicated pacifists, they refuse to fight in any war.

Anabaptist diversity is nearly as great as the general diversity of Christianity itself. Less conservative Anabaptists accept government benefits and serve in the military; members of stricter groups do neither (though all pay taxes). Although some use technology in business and agriculture, the conservative Swartzentruber Amish have gone to jail rather than affix reflectors to their buggies.

FRIENDS

In the early 1650s, some 60 independent-thinking English Puritans reached a radical conclusion for the day: direct experience of the light of Christ was universally possible regardless of clergy, sacrament, or church. Founded by George Fox, they soon organized as the Religious Society of Friends. Their worship was centered on the Meeting (congregation), where silent prayer was combined with preaching and testimony. Outsiders began calling them Quakers due to their emotional way of trembling when giving their testimony of faith. They believed in pacifism and refused to take part in warlike actions.

While the Friends were originally mocked as "Quakers," most today have embraced the term. Oliver Cromwell's Puritans, not known for their warm tolerance or rollicking sense of fun, threw many Friends in jail. From that prison experience stems the longtime Quaker sympathy with inhumane jail conditions—a tradition of social activism that would become, after worship, a second raison d'être of the Quaker faith.

By 1656, Friends had begun moving to North America. Unfortunately for them, the Massachusetts Bay Colony, like England, was in Puritan hands. Many Friends were jailed and abused. Most moved to less hostile Colonial areas: Rhode Island, New Jersey, Delaware, Maryland, and especially Pennsylvania. It didn't take long for the plight of the slaves to trouble the collective Quaker conscience, and Friends were early rejecters of the "peculiar institution." They wouldn't have countenanced war to free slaves, but from the Quaker standpoint, if ever a wrong spawned a right, it was the Civil War, since it led to the abolition of slavery.

Many of today's 380,000 Quakers live in the United States, England, and Kenya. Unlike many Anabaptists, Quakers don't live apart from society. You'll find them active in all professions and volunteering in numerous organizations that promote peace and human rights.

Culture and History of the Cherokee

When 16th-century European explorers first began surveying what would later be called the United States, they found a land already inhabited by a variety of groups. Among these were a people living in the southeast corner of the continent who referred to themselves as the *Aniyunwiya*, or "the principal people." Their Creek Indian neighbors, however, called them the *Tsalagi*, and the white tongue morphed that word into Cherokee, the name generally used today.

The origin of the Cherokee is uncertain. Tribal legend speaks of an ancient time of migration, which some historians have projected as far back as the time of a land bridge linking North America to Asia. Linguists report that the Cherokee language is linked to the Iroquois, who lived far to the north; others point out that traditional Cherokee crafts bear a resemblance to those of the people of the Amazon basin in South America. Regardless of their origin, the Cherokee held sway over a great deal of land when Spaniard Hernando de Soto made contact with the tribe in the 1540s.

De Soto did not find the gold he was looking for in Cherokee territory. What he did find was a people who had heard of his treatment of other tribes and did everything they could to hasten his exit from their land. They quickly traded him some food and other supplies—including two buffalo skins, the first European contact with the animal, which at the time ranged as far east as the Atlantic coast—and suggested that he might be better off looking to the west. With that, de Soto headed off. The total number de Soto found living in their traditional lands is a matter of speculation; the oldest reliable count dates from 130 years later, long after the smallpox the Spaniard left behind had wreaked havoc on the tribe. The disease left somewhere between 25,000 and 50,000 people alive after killing an estimated 75 percent of the native population.

CULTURE SHOCK

The Cherokee soon realized that the white intruders were there to stay, and they did what they could to adapt to the changing world. On the arrival of the British, they became active trading partners, seeking to improve their situation through the acquisition of European goods and guns. They also became military allies—by many accounts, a trade at which they excelled—fighting with the British against the French and later against the Colonists in the American Revolution.

The British, however, always viewed their Cherokee allies with suspicion, the effects of which ranged from the occasional massacre to the imposition of treaties demanding that the British be allowed to construct forts in Cherokee territory. This ceding of property was only the beginning of one of the biggest land-grabs in history, culminating in the 1838 Trail of Tears, in which 17,000 Cherokee were forcibly sent west. Thousands died during their forlorn trek.

Part of the difficulty with the early treaties was that the Europeans were in the habit of making them with anyone who claimed they represented the tribe; in reality, nobody could speak for all of the Cherokee. Their system was one of local autonomous government, with each village being responsible for its own affairs. The individual villages even had two chiefs: a White Chief in charge of domestic decisions and a Red Chief in charge of war and general relations with outsiders. The society was matrilineal and focused on a spiritual balance that the Cherokee believed existed between lower and higher worlds, with the earth caught in the middle. Europeans were ill-suited to understanding such a culture.

THE TIMES, THEY ARE A-CHANGIN'

Cherokee society proved up to the challenge, however. Part of the advance was because of Sequoyah. Sequoyah was a silversmith who devised the first syllabary for the Cherokee language in 1821. Although Sequoyah was illiterate, he had observed the white man's system of written communication. His Talking Leaves system, consisting of more than 80 symbols that each represented a syllable of Cherokee speech, was rapidly adopted; soon the Cherokee had a higher literacy rate than most of their white neighbors. One immediate result was the publication of a newspaper, *The Cherokee Phoenix*, in

1828; it was soon renamed the *Cherokee Phoenix and Indian Advocate* to indicate that its pages addressed issues faced by all Native Americans.

The 1820s proved a time of change for Cherokee society as a whole. The Cherokee unified their autonomous tribes by the close of the decade. They adopted a constitution that provided for a formal judiciary and elected legislature, electing John Ross as principal chief and declaring themselves to be an independent nation. They took the nearly unheard-of step of sending Indian representatives to Washington, D.C., to persuade Congress and the Supreme Court that the United States ought to be held to both the spirit as well as the letter of various treaties that were signed over the years. Despite impressing many with the quality of their arguments, their efforts proved fruitless. The Cherokee were treated as second-class citizens for decades to come.

The repercussions from the almost unimaginable changes imposed on the Cherokee as European settlers came to dominate the continent echo to the current day. However, Cherokee society has proved itself equal to the task, and today its people are the most numerous of any Native American population. The leadership of various parts of the tribe continues to actively work to remedy past inequities.

Lieutenant Vernon Baker and the Buffalo Soldiers

Of the almost one million African Americans who were either drafted or voluntarily enlisted in the U.S. Army during World War II, only one all-black Army division experienced infantry combat in Europe—the 92nd Infantry Division.

During the war, most African American soldiers were relegated to duty as cooks, clerks, and other positions in rear-echelon units. The military, like much of American society at the time, was segregated. But in 1941—after years of pressure from civil rights advocates—the U.S. federal government rescinded official policy that had excluded African Americans from combat duty.

BRING BACK THE BUFFALO SOLDIERS

Under the new policy, the 92nd Infantry Division was reactivated in October 1942. (The original 92nd Infantry Division was activated in October 1917. The all-black unit was sent overseas in July 1918 and saw action in the Meuse-Argonne Offensive, one of the last big military battles of World War I.)

The 92nd Infantry Division of World War II was a segregated unit composed of mostly Southern black enlisted men and junior officers under the exclusive command of white senior officers. Most of the enlisted men in the unit could neither read nor write.

The men of the 92nd maintained a proud tradition started by members of their World War I unit—they retained the buffalo as their divisional insignia. (Native Americans originated the "buffalo soldiers" term in 1866, in reference to the 9th and 10th black U.S. cavalry regiments.) The design featured a black buffalo in silhouette against an olive background. The 92nd kept a buffalo as its mascot and even named its newsletter after the animal.

The unit was sent overseas, disembarking in Naples, Italy, on July 30, 1944. Shortly after coming ashore, members of the 92nd first experienced combat when they faced off against German Field Marshal Albert Kesselring's troops at the infamous Gothic Line—a series of fortifications across the northern part of the Italian peninsula. One component of the 92nd, the 370th Regimental Combat Team, had its first taste of combat in September 1944 near the Arno River. By midmonth, the all-black regiment had managed to drive the defenders to the base of the Apennines mountain range.

VALOR IN ACTION: LIEUTENANT VERNON BAKER

Vernon Joseph Baker was born in Cheyenne, Wyoming, on December 17, 1919. Tired of being what he called a "servant," Baker quit his job as a railroad porter and enlisted in the Army on June 26, 1941. He was later assigned to the 370th Regimental Combat Team.

On April 5 and 6, 1945, Lieutenant Baker led his weapons platoon, as well as three rifle platoons, in an attack on a German stronghold at Castle Aghinolfi near Viareggio, Italy. During the patrol, Baker managed to kill nine Germans single-handedly and destroy three machine-gun positions, an observation post, and a dugout. The following evening Baker led an advance patrol through minefields.

During the engagement, Baker claimed his white company commander abandoned him. When he returned to regimental headquarters to deliver the dog tags of the 19 men killed during the patrol, Baker later recounted being "chewed out by the regimental commander Colonel Sherman himself, because I wasn't wearing a steel helmet."

Lieutenant Vernon Baker was originally passed over for a Medal of Honor. He was awarded the Distinguished Service Cross for his actions. However, a 1992 study commissioned by the

U.S. Army discovered "systematic racial discrimination in the criteria for awarding medals" during the war. The study recommended several African American recipients of the Distinguished Service Cross, including Baker, be upgraded to the Medal of Honor. He received the highest military award from President Bill Clinton in a ceremony held at the White House on January 13, 1997. Of the seven African Americans so honored at the ceremony, Baker was the only living recipient.

RECOGNITION FOR SERVICE

The 370th fought German and Italian units throughout the Serchio River Valley in Tuscany and finished the war in the Ligurian city of Genoa. During the Italian campaign, 2,848 soldiers of the Buffalo Division lost their lives. These gallant African American soldiers captured or helped capture some 24,000 enemy soldiers and, in return for their gallant conduct on the battlefield, received more than 12,000 decorations and citations.

Segregation in the military ended officially on July 26, 1948, when President Harry Truman issued Executive Order 9981. The order declared that "there shall be equality of treatment and opportunity for all persons in the armed services without regard to race, color, religion, or national origin."

THE "TUSKEGEE AIRMEN" TAKE TO THE SKIES

One of the first groups of African Americans to see action in World War II were the "Tuskegee Airmen." In June 1943, pilots from the 332nd Fighter Group conducted a dive-bombing mission against German units on the Italian island of Pantelleria. Battling the *Luftwaffe* throughout the war, the 332nd racked up an impressive record. They flew more than 15,000 sorties, often escorting bombers to their targets. In all, they downed 109 *Luftwaffe* planes.

Freemasons

For many, talk of "Freemasonry" conjures up images of intricate handshakes, strange rituals, and harsh punishment for revealing secrets about either. In actuality, the roots of the order are brotherhood and generosity. Throughout the ages, Masons have been known to fiercely protect their members and the unique features of their society.

The fantastically named Most Ancient and Honorable Society of Free and Accepted Masons began like other guilds; it was a collection of artisans brought together by their common trade, in this case, stone cutting and crafting. (There are many speculations as to when the society first began. Some believe it dates back to when King Solomon's temple was built. Others believe the guild first formed in Scotland in the 16th century.) The Freemasons made the welfare of their members a priority. Group elders devised strict work regulations for masons, whose skills were always in demand and were sometimes taken advantage of.

Organized Freemasonry emerged in Great Britain in the mid-17th century with the firm establishment of Grand Lodges and smaller, local Lodges. (No one overarching body governs Freemasonry as a whole, though lodges worldwide are usually linked either to England or France.) In 1730, transplanted Englishmen established the first American Lodge in Virginia, followed in 1733 by the continent's first chartered and opened Grand Lodge in Massachusetts. Boasting early American members including George Washington, Benjamin Franklin, and John Hancock, Freemasonry played a part in the growth of the young nation in ways that gradually attracted curiosity, speculation, and concern.

The source of the organization's mysterious reputation lay partly in its secrecy: Masons were prohibited from revealing secrets (some believed Masons would be violently punished if they revealed secrets, though the Masons deny such rumors). The Masonic bond also emphasized a commitment to one another. Outsiders feared the exclusivity smacked of conspiracy and compromised the motives of Masons appointed to juries or elected to public office. And nonmembers wondered about the meanings of the Freemasons' peculiar traditions (such as code words and other secretive forms of recognition between members) and symbolism (often geometric shapes or tools, such as the square and compass). Design elements of the one-dollar bill, including the Great Seal and the "all-seeing eye," have been credited to founding fathers such as Charles Thomson and other Masons.

Freemasonry in the United States suffered a serious blow in September 1826 when New York Masons abducted a former "brother" named William Morgan. Morgan was about to publish a book of Masonic secrets, but before he could, he was instead ushered north to the Canadian border and, in all likelihood, thrown into the Niagara River. His disappearance led to the arrest and conviction of three men on kidnapping charges (Morgan's body was never found)—scant penalties, locals said, for crimes that surely included murder. The affair increased widespread suspicion of the brotherhood, spawning an American Anti-Mason movement and even a new political party dedicated to keeping Freemasons out of national office.

In the decades following the Civil War, men were again drawn to brotherhood and fellowship as they searched for answers in a changing age, and Freemasonry slowly regained popularity. Today, Freemasonry remains an order devoted to its own members, charitable causes, and the betterment of society. It has a worldwide membership of at least five million. Its members are traditionally male, though certain associations now permit women. Despite the name, most members are not stonemasons. They are, however, required to have faith in a supreme being, but not necessarily the Christian god (Mohammed, Buddha, and so forth are all acceptable).

CHAPTER 7

LET'S HEAR IT FOR THE LADIES!

American Women Get the Vote

Between 1818 and 1820, Fanny Wright lectured throughout the United States on women's issues. Little did she know that it would take another 100 years for American women to achieve the right to vote.

THE BEGINNING

Margaret Brent, a landowner in Maryland, was the very first woman in the United States to call for voting rights. In 1647, Brent insisted on two votes in the colonial assembly—one for herself and one for the man for whom she held power of attorney. The governor rejected her request.

Then there was Abigail Adams. In 1776, she wrote to her husband, John, asking him to remember the ladies in the new laws he was drafting. Her husband did not take her request seriously, however.

Almost half a century later, Fanny Wright showed up from Scotland. Although she recognized the gender inequities in the United States, she nonetheless fell in love with the country and became a naturalized citizen in 1825.

It wasn't until the 1840s that the feminist ball really got rolling. Because progress was achieved in fits and spurts, women's suffrage took the better part of a century to come to fruition.

PROGRESS

Before the Civil War, the women's suffrage movement and abolition organizations focused on many of the same issues. The two movements were closely linked, specifically at the World Anti-Slavery Convention in London in 1840. However, female delegates to the convention, among them Lucretia Mott and Elizabeth Cady Stanton, were not allowed to participate because of their gender. London is a long way to travel to sit in the back of a room and be silent; Stanton and Mott resolved to organize a convention to discuss the rights of women.

The convention was finally held in 1848 in Seneca Falls, New York. Stanton presented her Declaration of Sentiments, the first formal action by women in the United States to advocate civil rights and suffrage.

Two groups formed at the end of the 1860s: the National Woman Suffrage Association (NWSA) and the American Woman Suffrage Association (AWSA). The NWSA, led by Susan B. Anthony and Stanton, worked to change voting laws on the federal level by way of an amendment to the U.S. Constitution. The AWSA, led by Lucy Stone and Julia Ward Howe, worked to change the laws on the state level. The two groups were united in 1890 and renamed the National American Woman Suffrage Association.

FULFILLMENT

In 1916, Alice Paul formed the National Woman's Party (NWP). Based on the idea that action, not words, would achieve the suffragists' mission, the NWP staged Silent Sentinels outside the White House during which NWP members held signs that goaded the president.

When World War I came along, many assumed the Silent Sentinels would end. Instead, the protesters incorporated the current events into their messages. Once the public got wind that some protestors had been imprisoned and were experiencing horrendous treatment, the tide turned in their favor.

In 1917, President Woodrow Wilson announced his support for a suffrage amendment. In the summer of 1920, Tennessee ratified the 19th Amendment—the 36th state to do so. In August of that year, women gained the right to vote. It had certainly been a long time coming.

Ms. President?

When Victoria Woodhull ran for president in 1872, some called her a witch, others said she was a prostitute. The idea of a woman even casting a vote for president was considered scandalous—which may explain why Woodhull spent election night in jail.

Known for her passionate speeches and fearless attitude, Victoria Woodhull became a trailblazer for women's rights. Woodhull advocated revolutionary ideas, including gender equality and women's voting rights. "Women are the equals of men before the law and are equal in all their rights," she said. America, however, wasn't ready to accept her "radical" ideas.

Woodhull was born in 1838 in Homer, Ohio, the seventh child of Annie and Buck Claflin. Her deeply spiritual mother often took little Victoria along to revival camps where people would speak in tongues. Her mother also dabbled in clairvoyance, and Victoria and her younger sister Tennessee believed they had a gift for it as well. With so many chores to do at home (washing, ironing, chipping wood, and cooking), Victoria only attended school sporadically and was primarily self-educated.

Soon after the family left Homer, a 28-year-old doctor named Canning Woodhull asked the 15-year-old Victoria for her hand in marriage. The marriage was no paradise for Victoria, who soon realized her husband was an alcoholic. She experienced more heartbreak when her son, Byron, was born with a mental disability. While she remained married to Canning, Victoria spent the next few years touring as a clairvoyant with her sister Tennessee. At that time, it was difficult for a woman to pursue divorce, but Victoria finally divorced her husband in 1864. Two years later she married Colonel James Blood, a Civil War veteran who believed in free love.

In 1866, Victoria and James moved to New York City. Spiritualism was then in vogue, and Victoria and Tennessee established a salon where they acted as clairvoyants and engaged in political discussions with their clientele. Among their first customers was Cornelius Vanderbilt, the wealthiest man in America.

A close relationship sprang up between Vanderbilt and the two attractive and intelligent young women. He advised them on business matters and gave them stock tips. When the stock market crashed in September 1869, Woodhull made a bundle buying instead of selling during the ensuing panic. That winter, she and Tennessee opened their own brokerage business. They were the first female stockbrokers in American history.

AIMING HIGH

Woodhull had more far-reaching ambitions, however. On April 2, 1870, she announced that she was running for president. In conjunction with her presidential bid, Woodhull and her sister started a newspaper, *Woodhull & Claflin's Weekly*, which highlighted women's issues. It was another breakthrough for the two since they were the first women to ever publish a weekly newspaper.

That was followed by another milestone: On January 11, 1871, Woodhull became the first woman ever to speak before a congressional committee. As she spoke before the House Judiciary Committee, she asked that Congress change its stance on whether women could vote. Woodhull's reasoning was elegant in its simplicity. She was not advocating a new constitutional amendment granting women the right to vote. Instead, she reasoned, women already had that right. The Fourteenth Amendment says that, "All persons born or naturalized in the United States . . . are citizens of the Unites States." Since voting is part of the definition of being a citizen, Woodhull argued, women, in fact, already possessed the right to vote. Woodhull, a persuasive speaker, actually swayed some congressmen to her point of view; the committee chairman, however, remained hostile to the idea of women's rights and made sure the issue never came to a floor vote.

Woodhull had better luck with the suffragists. In May 1872, before 668 delegates from 22 states, Woodhull was chosen as the presidential candidate of the Equal Rights Party; she was the first woman ever chosen by a political party to run for president. But her presidential bid soon foundered. Woodhull was on record as an advocate of free love, which opponents argued was an attack on the institution of marriage.

That year, Woodhull caused an uproar when her newspaper ran an exposé about the infidelities of Reverend Henry Ward Beecher. Woodhull and her sister were thrown in jail and accused of publishing libel and promoting obscenity. They would spend election night of 1872 behind bars as Ulysses Grant defeated Horace Greeley for the presidency.

Woodhull was eventually cleared of the charges against her (the claims against Beecher were proven true), but hefty legal bills and a downturn in the stock market left her impoverished and embittered. She moved to England in 1877, shortly after divorcing Colonel Blood. By the turn of the century she had become wealthy once more, this time by marriage to a British banker. Fascinated by technology, she joined the Ladies Automobile Club, where her passion for automobiles led Woodhull to one last milestone: In her sixties, she and her daughter Zula became the first women to drive through the English countryside.

Catherine de' Medici

Speculation still swirls around the life of the Italian queen. She was said to be a poisoner and a sorceress— the sole instigator of a horrible massacre. She was also said to be a clever woman doing the best she could in difficult circumstances. Which is true?

◆ The daughter of Lorenzo the "Magnificent" and a French princess, Catherine was orphaned as an infant. Her mother died 15 days after Catherine's birth, and her father died six days later.

◈ The Medicis were overthrown in Florence when Catherine was eight years old, and she was taken hostage and moved from convent to convent around the city. She was often threatened with death or with life in a brothel to ruin her value as a bride.

◈ As was common at the time, Catherine was only 14 when she married Henri II. The match was arranged by her uncle, Pope Clement VII, and Henri's father, François I, king of France.

◈ Catherine spent her married life overlooked in favor of Henri's lifelong mistress, Diane de Poiters, the Duchesse de Valentinois. Even at Catherine's coronation, Diane was publicly honored as well.

◈ Henri and Catherine didn't have children for the first ten years of their union, but at the insistence of Diane, the couple finally consummated their marriage. They eventually had ten children.

◈ Catherine supposedly saw a vision of Henri's death days before it happened. She begged him not to joust at the tournament held in celebration of their daughter Elisabeth's marriage to Philip II of Spain. He did so anyway and died from an eye infection caused by a splinter from a broken lance.

◈ After Henri died, Catherine wore mourning clothes for the rest of her life. She also took a broken lance as her emblem, bearing the motto "From this come my tears and my pain."

◈ Once out from under Henri's and Diane's influence, Catherine spread her wings and began to exercise control over her children. She ruled France as regent during the minority of Charles IX (and continued to rule during his adulthood, though as the king's "advisor" rather than regent), and Henri III relied heavily on her throughout his reign.

◈ The Medici family, though very wealthy, was a merchant family rather than nobility. Catherine was reviled by many of the French because she was thought to be a commoner and, therefore, in their eyes, unfit to be queen of France.

◈ Despite her reputation as a persecutor of Protestants, Catherine actually tried to compromise between the Catholic and Protestant factions. She made concessions to Protestants, allowing them to worship their own way in private, but war broke out nonetheless.

◈ Though she is often blamed for the St. Bartholomew's Day Massacre, it is not known what role Catherine played in the disaster. Some historians believe she intended it only to be a culling of Protestant nobles who had been leaders against her in the religious wars, but the situation got out of control.

◈ Among Catherine's ten children were three kings of France (François II, Charles IX, and Henri III, respectively) and two queens: Margaret, called Margot, married Henri of Navarre, and Elisabeth became Queen of Spain.

◈ François II, Catherine's eldest son, was married to Mary, Queen of Scots.

◈ Tragically, Catherine's large brood turned out to be sickly, and she outlived all but two of her ten children. Three had died in infancy, and only Henri and Margot were still alive when Catherine died.

She Struck Out DiMaggio

It was the most unusual of baseball showdowns. Two of the 20th century's greatest sports icons stared each other down across a distance of 60 feet, 6 inches. At the plate: Yankee legend Joe DiMaggio. On the mound: a woman.

But this was no ordinary woman. She was, perhaps, the greatest female athlete of all time. Babe Didrikson Zaharias had been throwing harder and running faster than the boys since she was a girl in Port Arthur, Texas. On this day, she was pitching for the barnstorming House of David men's team.

The details of this legendary face-off between DiMaggio and Zaharias have become cloudy with the passage of time. However, DiMaggio once described it to writer Bert Sugar. "Struck him out on three pitches," Sugar said.

Born Mildred Ella Didrikson, Babe earned her nickname after a Ruthian feat: smashing five home runs during a childhood game. Baseball was not even her best sport. She set Olympic records at the 1932 Games, winning the javelin and breaking a world record in the 80-meter hurdles. She was also a basketball star, a world-class swimmer, and—above all else—a brilliant golfer whose titles included the 1948, 1950, and 1954 United States Women's Opens.

In 1934, Zaharias pitched in two major-league spring training games in Florida. She threw the first inning of a Philadelphia Athletics match against Brooklyn, walking one batter but not allowing a hit. Two days later, she pitched an inning for the Cardinals against the Red Sox, yielding her first runs. She did not bat in either game, but in warm-ups she reportedly chucked a baseball from center field to home plate—a distance of 313 feet.

12 Renowned Women of the Wild West

Perhaps no other time in America's history is as steeped in myth, legend, and adventure as the pioneering age of the "Wild West." Outlaws, lawmen, cowboys, American Indians, miners, ranchers, and more than a few "ladies of ill repute" emerged in this era, from 1865 to 1900. Any female settler in the West was a heroine in her own right, but listed here are a few of the more famous (and infamous) women of this intriguing period.

1. Annie Oakley: Probably the best-known woman of the Wild West, Annie Oakley was born Phoebe Ann Oakley Moses in Dark County, Ohio, in 1860, and she was shooting like a pro by age 12. Germany's Kaiser Wilhelm II trusted her with a gun so much that he let her shoot the ash off his cigarette while he smoked it. Oakley is the only woman of the Wild West to have a Broadway musical loosely based on her life (*Annie Get Your Gun*), which

depicts her stint in Buffalo Bill's famous traveling show. When she joined the show, Bill touted her as "Champion Markswoman." When she died in 1926, it was discovered that her entire fortune had been spent on various charities, including women's rights and children's services.

2. Belle Starr: Myra Maybelle Shirley Reed Starr was born in Carthage, Missouri, in 1848. Frank and Jesse James's gang hid out at her family's farm when she was a kid, and from then on, she was hooked on the outlaw life. Later, when her husband Jim Reed shot a man, the two went on the run, robbing banks and counterfeiting. Starr—who was known to wear feathers in her hair, buckskins, and a pistol on each hip—was shot in the back while riding her horse in 1889. It's still unclear whether her death was an accident or murder.

3. Charley Parkhurst: Times were rough for ladies in the Wild West, so this crackerjack stagecoach driver decided to live most of her life as a man. Born Charlotte Darkey Parkhurst in 1812, she lived well into her sixties, in spite of being a hard-drinking, tobacco-chewing, fearless, one-eyed brute. She drove stages (not an easy or particularly safe career) for Wells Fargo and the California Stage Company. Using her secret identity, Parkhurst was a registered voter and may have been the first American woman to cast a ballot. She lived out her later years raising cattle and chickens. After she died in 1879, her true identity was revealed, much to the surprise of her friends.

4. Calamity Jane: Born Martha Jane Canary in Missouri around 1856, Calamity Jane was a sharpshooter by the time she was a young woman. She received her nickname, Calamity Jane, when she rescued an army captain in South Dakota after their camp was attacked by Native Americans. Jane was said to be a whiskey-drinking, "don't-mess-with-me" kind of gal. She is reported to have saved the lives of six stagecoach passengers in 1876 when they were attacked by Native Americans, and she joined Buffalo Bill's show in the mid-1890s. Though she married a man named Burk at age 33, when Jane died in 1903, she asked to be buried next to Wild Bill Hickock. Rumor has it that Hickock was the only man she ever loved.

5. Josephine Sarah Marcus: A smolderingly good-looking actor born in 1861, Marcus came to Tombstone, Arizona, while touring with a theater group performing Gilbert & Sullivan's *H.M.S. Pinafore*. She stuck around as mistress to Sheriff John Behan, but when Wyatt Earp showed up, her relationship with Behan went cold, and she and Earp reportedly fell in love. Josephine passed away in 1944 and claimed until her dying day that Wyatt Earp was her one and only true love.

6. Laura Bullion: More commonly referred to as "Rose of the Wild Bunch," this outlaw was born around 1876 in Knickerbocker, Texas, and learned the outlaw trade by observing her bank-robbing father. Eventually hooking up with Butch Cassidy and his Wild Bunch, Bullion fenced money for the group and became romantically involved with several members. Most of those men died by the gun, but "The Thorny Rose" gave up her life of crime after serving time in prison. She died a respectable seamstress in Memphis, Tennessee, in 1961.

7. Etta Place: Like many women of the Wild West, Etta Place's life is shrouded in mystery and legend. Was she a schoolteacher who left her quiet life for the drama of the outlaw life? Was she Butch Cassidy's girlfriend? Was she in love with the Sundance Kid, or were they just friendly cousins? Evidence seems to indicate that Place was born around 1878 and became a prostitute at Fanny Porter's bordello in San Antonio, Texas. When the Wild Bunch came through, Place went with them to rob banks. She wasn't with the boys when they were killed in South America in 1909; some believe she became a cattle rustler, but no one really knows for sure.

8. Lillian Smith: Before Tonya Harding and Nancy Kerrigan, there was the rivalry between this sharpshooter and her nemesis, Annie Oakley. Born in 1871, Smith joined Buffalo Bill's show at age 15 and was notorious for wearing flashy clothes, cursing like a sailor, and bragging about her superior skills. When the show went to England in 1887, Smith shot poorly and was ridiculed, while Oakley rose to the occasion. This crushing blow put Smith behind Oakley in the history books, and she died in 1930, a relatively obscure relic of the Old West.

9. Pearl de Vere: One of the most famous madams in history, this red-haired siren was born in Indiana around 1860 and made her way to Colorado during the Silver Panic of 1893. De Vere told her family she was a dress designer, but in fact rose to fame as the head of the Old Homestead, a luxurious brothel in Cripple Creek, Colorado. The price of a night's stay could cost patrons more than $200—at a time when most hotels charged around $3 a night! The building was reportedly equipped with an intercom system and boasted fine carpets and chandeliers. De Vere died in 1897 after a huge party at the Old Homestead. An overdose of morphine killed her, but it is unclear whether it was accidental or not.

10. Ellen Liddy Watson: Also known as "Cattle Kate," this lady of the West made a name for herself in the late 1800s when she was in her mid-twenties. Watson worked as a cook in the Rawlins House hotel and there she met her true love, James Averell. The two were hanged in 1889 by vigilantes who claimed Averell and Watson were cattle rustlers. It is now believed that their murder was unjustified, however—the result of an abuse of power by land and cattle owners.

11. Pearl Hart: Pearl Hart was born in Canada around 1870, but by the time she was 17, she was married to a gambler and on a train to America. She especially liked life in the West, and, at 22, tried to leave her husband to pursue opportunities there. Her husband followed her and won her back, but Hart was already living it up with cigarettes, liquor, and even morphine. After her husband left to fight in the Spanish-American War, Hart met a man named Joe Boot, and they robbed stagecoaches for a while before she was caught and jailed. Hart is famous for saying, "I shall not consent to be tried under a law in which my sex had no voice in making." She was eventually released, but the rest of her life is unknown.

12. Rose Dunn: In a family of outlaws, it was only a matter of time before "The Rose of Cimarron" was working in the business, too. Dunn met Doolin Gang member George Newcomb and joined him as he and his crew robbed stagecoaches and banks. During a particularly nasty gunfight, Dunn risked her life to supply Newcomb with a gun and bullets. She then helped him escape after he was wounded in battle. Dunn died around 1950 in her mid-seventies, a respectable citizen married to a local politician.

Killer Queens

When playwright William Congreve wrote, "Hell hath no fury like a woman scorned," he may have had these warrior queens in mind.

BOUDICCA (A.D. 61)—NEMESIS OF NERO

She stood six feet tall, sported a hip-length mane of fiery red hair, and had a vengeful streak a mile wide. She was Boudicca, queen of the Celtic Iceni people of eastern Britain. In A.D. 61, she led a furious uprising against the occupying Romans that nearly chased Nero's legions from the island.

Boudicca didn't always hate the Romans. The Iceni kingdom, led by her husband, Prasutagus, was once a Roman ally. But Prasutagus lived a life of conspicuous wealth on borrowed Roman money, and when it came time to pay the piper, he was forced to bequeath half his kingdom to the Romans; the other half was left for his daughters.

The Romans, however, got greedy; on Prasutagus's death, they moved to seize all Iceni lands as payment for the dead king's debt. When the widow Boudicca challenged the Romans, they publicly flogged her and raped her daughters. While most of the Roman army in Britain was busy annihilating the Druids in the west, the scorned Boudicca led the Iceni and other aggrieved Celtic peoples on a bloody rebellion that reverberated all the way back to Rome.

Boudicca's warriors annihilated the vaunted Roman Ninth Legion and laid waste to the Roman cities of Camulodunum (Colchester), Londinium (London), and Verulamium (St. Albans). Boudicca's vengeance knew no bounds and was exacted on both Romans and fellow Britons who supported them. Upwards of 80,000 people fell victim to her wrath.

The Romans were floored by the ferocity of Boudicca's attack, and Nero actually considered withdrawing his army from Britain. But the Romans regrouped, and later a seasoned force of 1,200 legionnaires trounced Boudicca's 100,000-strong rebel army in a decisive battle. The defeated Boudicca chose suicide by poison over capture.

Today, a statue of the great Boudicca can be found near Westminster Pier in London, testament to the veneration the British still hold for Boudicca as their first heroine.

EMPRESS JINGO (A.D. 169–269)—PERSUADER OF GODS AND MEN

She led the Japanese in the conquest of Korea in the early 3rd century. In 1881, she became the first woman to be featured on a Japanese banknote—no small feat given the chauvinism of imperial Japan. More than 1,700 years after her rule, Empress Jingo is still revered in Japan.

Perhaps Jingo's success as a warrior queen can be attributed to the irresistible sway she held over both the ancient deities and mortal men. As regent ruler of imperial Japan following the death of her emperor husband, Chuai, Jingo was determined to make Korea her own. According to Japanese lore, she beguiled Ryujin, the Japanese dragon god of the sea, to lend her his magical Tide Jewels, which she used to create favorable tides that destroyed the Korean fleet and safely guided the Japanese fleet to the Korean peninsula. From there, she commanded and cajoled her armies to an illustrious campaign of conquest that secured her exalted status in Japanese history.

Jingo purportedly had amazing powers of persuasion over the human reproductive cycle as well. Pregnant with Chuai's son at the time of the invasion, Jingo remained in Korea for the duration of the campaign, which by all accounts lasted well beyond the length of a normal pregnancy term. Legend has it, however, that she delayed giving birth until after the conquest so that her son and heir, Ojin, could be born in Japan.

Once home, Jingo cemented her power by using brute force to convince several rivals to the throne to concede to her rule, which would last for more than 60 years.

ZENOBIA (A.D. 274)—MISTRESS OF THE MIDDLE EAST

Like Boudicca before her, the warrior queen Zenobia made her name by leading an army against the mighty Romans. Unlike the Celtic queen, however, Zenobia would experience a much different fate.

Zenobia and her husband, Odenathus, ruled the prosperous Syrian city of Palmyra. Though technically subordinate to Odenathus, she certainly didn't take a backseat to him. She established herself as a warrior queen by riding at her husband's side into battle against the Persians—often overshadowing her more reserved mate by shouting loud battle cries, walking for miles within the ranks of the foot soldiers, and drinking the boys under the table in victory celebrations.

Zenobia became the undisputed ruler of Palmyra in 267 following the assassination of Odenathus (which some attribute to Zenobia herself). As an ostensible ally of Rome, Zenobia launched a campaign of conquest in the Middle East, leading, walking, and drinking with her men as always. Within three years she expanded her realm to Syria, Egypt, and much of Asia Minor.

Flushed with success, Zenobia declared Palmyra's independence from Rome. But in 272, the Romans struck back. Zenobia was up for the fight, but her forces were overextended. The Romans easily recaptured Zenobia's outlying territories before laying siege to Palmyra itself.

After its fall, Palmyra was destroyed, and Zenobia was captured. She was taken to Rome and paraded in golden chains before Emperor Aurelian. But even in defeat, Zenobia triumphed. The striking beauty with the defiant stride struck a chord with Aurelian, who later pardoned her and allowed her to live a life of luxury on an estate outside Rome.

AETHELFLAED (A.D. 869–918)—"NOBLE BEAUTY" OF THE ANGLO-SAXONS

In England at the beginning of the 10th century, the Anglo kingdom of Wessex and the Saxon kingdom of

Mercia were both under siege by the Danish Vikings. The cocksure Vikings were confident of victory, but they hadn't counted on the rise of the Mercian queen, Aethelflaed (her name means "noble beauty"), who would earn her warrior reputation by leading her armies in victory over the Vikings and emerging as one of Britain's most powerful rulers.

Aethelflaed's father, Alfred the Great, was king of Wessex. Aethelflaed, at age 15, married the Mercian nobleman Ethelred, thus forming a strategic alliance of the two kingdoms against the Vikings. Her first fight against the Vikings occurred on her wedding day, when the Norsemen tried to kill her to prevent the nuptial and political union. Aethelflaed took up the sword and fought alongside her guards while holed up in an old trench, eventually driving the Vikings away.

From then on, battling Vikings became old hat for Aethelflaed. When her husband died in 911, she assumed sole rule of Mercia and began taking the fight to the Vikings. Perhaps remembering her wedding-day experience in the trench, she built formidable fortifications to defend Mercia. She also used exceptional diplomatic skills to form alliances against the Vikings. By the time of her death in 918, she had led her armies in several victories over the Vikings, had them begging for peace, and had extended her power in Britain.

Aethelflaed made her name as a Viking killer, but her most important legacy was her success in sustaining the union of the Angles and the Saxons, which would later germinate into the English nation.

Sarah Emma Edmonds (aka Frank Thompson)

This patriotic and devoted woman was determined to fight for her country—even if it meant posing as a man.

During the Civil War, women, their hearts full of worry and sorrow, watched their husbands, brothers, and sons march away to the battlefield. While such emotional partings were difficult, some women also felt deep regret that they couldn't suit up to defend their country as well. The life of the average woman in the 1860s was one of restrictions and clearly defined gender roles: They were to maintain the home and raise the children. Joining the military certainly was not an option. Still, as many as 400 women snuck into brigades from both North and South by posing as male soldiers. Some successfully maintained their disguise, while others were discovered and discharged for "sexual incompatibility." These female soldiers were trailblazers who put their lives on the line for their beliefs.

Sarah Emma Edmonds, born in 1841, believed that everyone should have the chance to fight for freedom and liberty—no matter what their gender. By age 17, she had already proven herself bold and willing to buck convention, fleeing her home in New Brunswick, Canada, to escape her overbearing father. She stole away in the night to create a new, unencumbered life for herself in the United States, settling in Flint, Michigan.

STARTING OVER

Edmonds knew that if she was going to experience the world in the way she wished, she'd have to reinvent herself entirely. As a woman, she could never fulfill her dreams of adventure—too many doors were closed to her on the basis of gender. But she believed those doors would open if she could become a man. Discarding the identity of Sarah Emma Edmonds, she became Franklin Thompson, a book salesman. Dressed as a man and acting with assertiveness and confidence, she was soon able to support herself independently. Edmonds saw America as a land of unlimited potential, and she was determined to make the most of it.

When war broke out, Edmonds saw another opportunity to prove her mettle and joined up with a Michigan infantry as a male nurse and courier. "I am naturally fond of adventure," she later explained, "a little ambitious and a good deal romantic and this together with my devotion to the Federal cause and determination to assist to the utmost of my ability in crushing the rebellion, made me forget the unpleasant items."

UPPING THE ANTE

Posing as Franklin Thompson, Edmonds blended in with the men of her unit, served admirably, and aroused no suspicions during her tour of duty. Since her disguise seemed to be working so well, she volunteered to spy for General George McClellan at the start of the Peninsula Campaign. Edmonds continued to be effective in her use of disguises. She infiltrated the Confederates at Yorktown as a black slave by darkening her skin with silver nitrate and wearing a wig. After several days there, she returned to McClellan and shared the information she had gained. Edmonds's next assignment found her portraying a heavyset Irish woman named Bridget O'Shea. As O'Shea, she crossed enemy lines, peddled her wares, and returned with an earful of Confederate secrets. In August 1862, Edmonds assumed the guise of a black laundress in a Confederate camp. One day, while washing an officer's jacket, she found a large packet of official papers. After giving the jacket a thorough "dry cleaning," Edmonds returned to Union camp with the packet.

THE GAME'S UP

All this time, army officials continued to believe Edmonds was Franklin Thompson. In the spring of 1863, she contracted malaria. She knew that she couldn't visit an army hospital for fear of being found out as a woman. She reluctantly slipped away to Cairo, Illinois, and checked into a private hospital. Although Edmonds had planned to return to her previous duty after her recovery, she discovered that during her sickness her alias, Private Thompson, had been pegged as a deserter. Edmonds couldn't reassume that identity without facing the consequences, and so she remained dressed as a woman and served as a nurse to soldiers in Washington, D.C.

AFTER THE FIGHTING STOPPED

Two years after the Civil War ended, she married Linus Seelye, a fellow Canadian expatriate. The couple eventually settled down in Cleveland, Ohio. Determined that the world know her story and see that a woman could fight just as well as a man, she wrote the best-selling *Nurse and Spy in the Union Army*, which exposed her gender-bending ways. She also fought hard for her alter ego, petitioning the War Department to expunge Frank Thompson's listing as a deserter. Following a War Department review of the case, Congress granted her service credit and a veteran's pension of $12 a month in 1884. She died five years later and was buried in the military section of a Houston cemetery.

High Priestess of the Cult of Peronismo

Long before cinema and media drama brought her back into North American eyes, the woman many called "Santa Evita" was a legend in her native land. Her memory now casts a shadow larger than life, which makes it hard to believe that she held influence for less than ten years and didn't live to be 35.

Is it "Eva" or "Evita"?
Eva liked the familiar version, which translates roughly to "Evie." It's like calling Lady Diana "Di."

What do we know about Evita's origin?
Eva María Ibarguren breathed her first on May 7, 1919, in Los Toldos, Argentina. Her mother, Juana, was involved with married estate manager Juan Duarte. Juana adopted Juan's last name for herself and her kids, but he soon went back to his wife in another town. When he died, Juana insisted on attending his funeral—scandalous, but the move hints at the origin of Evita's own strength

and bravery. Juana's family endured small-town whispers, breeding in young Eva much contempt for the stratified Argentine social order.

How did Evita find her way to greater things?
Early on, Evita was a thin, quiet, often truant girl. Acting in a school play convinced her she wanted a career in show business, so she headed to Buenos Aires. She was a hit at theater, movies, and radio acting, making herself one of

Argentina's best-paid actresses by 1943. Her stage presence and sense of public opinion would come in handy later in life.

Then came Juan Perón.

Argentina, theoretically democratic, was ruled by a series of oligarchies. Some were better, some worse, some in between. El coronel and widower Juan Domingo Perón was an influential soldier involved in politics, normal for the Argentine military of the day. In 1944, with Perón serving in the military government, an Andean earthquake devastated San Juan. Perón organized a benefit performance, and there he met Evita Duarte.

Fireworks?

For both. She soon moved in with him; their mutual love shows in all they did.

And that brought her into politics?

Evita left acting to lend her influential voice to peronismo, a cultlike mix of populism, nationalism, and authoritarianism. In effect, she became its high priestess.

So, Perón vaulted her into power?

Or perhaps Evita vaulted Perón into a position of power. Evita Duarte was influential independent of and before Juan Perón; he didn't make her. They were a mutually complementary political dream team.

When did Evita become Señora Dictator?

Perón's government enemies arrested him in October 1945. The peronista masses rallied, and the ruling junta yielded in time to save itself. Reunited with his jubilant partner, Juan planned to run for president. One problem: They were still living in sin. Evita became Señora Eva Duarte de Perón in a private civil ceremony. On June 4, 1946, Perón was elected president of Argentina.

Good deal for Evita?

Yes—but it also polarized perceptions of her. Argentina knew her well from Juan's campaign trail. To peronistas, Evita was the caring face of the movement. For anti-peronistas (now keeping low profiles), she was the upstart soap opera harlot, living high on the hog.

Which is more accurate?

The space between the extremes called her a "strong, smart woman." She did live far better than the impoverished descamisados ("shirtless") she championed. Monastic heads of state, or spouses of same, are rare anywhere. But she was wealthy and popular before peronismo, and her affinity for the downtrodden rings genuine given her upbringing. By building her husband's personality cult, she built her own. She held a political religion in the palm of her hand, and she learned to wield it with gutsy skill.

What else did she do?

Argentine women got the vote in 1947. *¿Coincidencia o Evita?*

In 1947, she also toured Europe, beginning with Franco's Spain. When the British didn't treat her visit as equal to one by Eleanor Roosevelt, Evita snubbed the U.K. Peronistas swelled with patriotism to see their defiant heroine on the world stage. Evita also founded a charity and a women's political party. By 1951, however, uterine cancer had begun to sap her strength.

Could the disease have been arrested if caught sooner?

Only Evita herself could tell us when she first felt something was wrong, but the physical impact is documented as early as 1950. By the time she underwent chemo and a radical hysterectomy, it was far too late. On July 26,

1952, Eva María Duarte de Perón, now anointed "Spiritual Leader of the Nation," passed from life to legend. Argentina wept bitter tears for her.

I heard that it didn't end with her death—some ghoulish story about embalming and a lost corpse. What really occurred?

Soon after she died, an embalmer did an outstanding job preserving Evita. She was supposed to be exhibited under glass in perpetuity, like Lenin. However, in 1955, a military coup booted Juan out of office—and out of Argentina. Peronismo was proscribed. Evita's body vanished.

Turns out she was interred in Milan, Italy, under an assumed name. In 1971, Evita was exhumed and sent to Juan's Spanish exile house, which in itself is a little macabre: "Excuse me, Señor, but that is my wife, not a coffee table." In 1973, Perón returned to Argentina to fan the *peronista* coals into a presidency. After his death in 1974, Evita Perón was reinterred in the securest possible crypt.

The heroine lay at last in the only true place that could give her rest: Argentina.

CHAPTER 8
HEALTH AND MEDICINE

Dance of the Black Death

The Black Death, the epidemic best known for devastating Europe between 1347 and 1350, was as deadly in the east as it was in the west. By the time the plague reached the outskirts of Europe, it had already killed an estimated 25 million people. Within three years, approximately 25 million more victims would follow in the first wave of a cycle of plagues that continued to hound Europe for three centuries.

The plague isn't pretty. Whether primarily in the lymph nodes (bubonic), blood (septicemic), or lungs (pneumonic), the plague is caused by the bacterium *Yersinia pestis*, which lives in the digestive tract of fleas. It primarily transmits from animals to humans through flea bites, though humans in close contact can transmit pneumonic plague to each other. The bacteria was discovered by Japanese and European researchers in the late 19th century. Patients manifest symptoms such as swollen and tender lymph nodes (buboes) in the area of the bite, fever, bloody sputum and blotching, rapidly worsening pneumonia, and—as the bacteria overwhelms the nervous system—

neurological and psychological disorders. Untreated, plague has a morbidity rate of 50–60 percent; the rate is even higher for pneumonic plague. Between 1,000 and 3,000 cases are reported each year worldwide.

ORIGINS OF A DISEASE

The Black Death originated in China in the 1340s. Making its way along the Silk Road, the epidemic ravaged India, Egypt, the Middle East, and Constantinople before spreading rapidly through trading ports to Europe. Even Greenland and Iceland were struck. From 1347 to 1350, a third of Europe's population died an agonizing, dramatic, mysterious—and sudden—death. In cities such as Florence, the death toll reached 75 percent, and many rural villages were wiped out completely. Nearly annual outbreaks of the plague continued, culminating in the great 1665 plague of London, in which perhaps 100,000 Londoners died. Overall, some estimates of the combined death toll reach 200 million people.

It would be hard to underestimate the pervasive effects of the plagues on Europe. All aspects of society and culture suffered intense disruption and experienced profound change as the plagues brought on economic stress, social dissolution, religious extremism, and skepticism. The trauma on the European psyche as a result of living in circumstances where, as the 14th-century Italian writer Boccaccio put it, people could "eat lunch with their friends and dinner with their ancestors in paradise," can be seen in the pervasive use of skeletons in art and drama. They act as grim and often ironic reminders of *memento mori* ("Remember, you die"), illustrations of *quod es fui, quod sum eris* ("what you are I was; what I am you will be"), and participants in the "Dance of Death" (*Danse Macabre, Totentanz*) throughout this period.

WAS THAT THE LAST DANCE?

Although the Black Death and its subsequent outbreaks ended in the 17th century, its rapid spread and descriptions, as well as the patterns of outbreaks do not—in some cases—correspond well to *Y. pestis*, nor to the complex conditions required for the bacteria to find its way into fleas that can then infect humans. This has recently led some researchers in Britain and the United States to advance the theory that the plague was actually caused by a human-borne virus that lies dormant in the earth until it is introduced into the population. If so, another round of "Black Death"—especially in an age of continuous global travel and trade—remains a frightening possibility.

Going for the Jugular

The human body has always been fertile ground for misconceptions.

The celebrated Greek doctor Hippocrates postulated that all human emotions flowed from four bodily fluids, or humors: blood (which makes you cheerful and passionate), yellow bile (which makes you hot-tempered), black bile (which makes you depressed), and phlegm (which makes you sluggish or stoic). Though the good doctor's humors have given behavioral scientists a nice structure for examining personality types (sanguine, choleric, melancholic, and phlegmatic), the idea that our bodily fluids make us angry, depressed, or elated died out in the 1800s.

The withering of the Hippocratic belief in humors proved to be good news for patients who were not thrilled with the practice of bloodletting, a process of opening a patient's veins to lower blood levels in an attempt to bring the humors into balance and cure all manner of mental and physical ills. Bloodletting, with a knife or with leeches, was an accepted medical practice from the time of the Greeks, Mayans, and Mesopotamians, and it was still going strong at the end of the 18th century, when George Washington had almost two liters of blood let out to "cure" a throat infection. (He died shortly afterward.)

12 Deadly Diseases Cured in the 20th Century

According to the U.S. Census Bureau, the average life expectancy at the beginning of the 20th century was 47.3 years. A century later, that number had increased to 77.85 years, due largely to the development of vaccinations and other treatments for deadly diseases. Of course, vaccines and treatments only work if they're given, which is why many of these diseases still persist in poorer, developing countries. Despite the success of vaccines, only one of these diseases—smallpox—has been erased from the globe. Here are 12 diseases that could be completely eradicated from the world if vaccines were made available to all.

1. Chicken Pox: Before 1995, a case of the chicken pox was a rite of passage for kids. The disease, caused by the *varicella-zoster* virus, creates an itchy rash of small red bumps on the skin. The virus spreads when someone who has the disease coughs or sneezes, and a nonimmune person inhales the viral particles. The virus can also be passed through contact with the fluid of chicken pox blisters. Most cases are minor but in more serious instances, chicken pox can trigger bacterial infections, viral pneumonia, and encephalitis (inflammation of the brain). According to the Centers for Disease Control and Prevention (CDC), before the chicken pox vaccine was approved for use in the United States in 1995, there were 11,000 hospitalizations and 100 deaths from the disease every year. Many countries do not require the vaccination because chicken pox doesn't cause that many deaths. They'd rather focus on vaccinating against the really serious diseases, so the disease is still common.

2. Diphtheria: Diphtheria is an infection of the bacteria *Corynebacterium diphtheriae* and mainly affects the nose and throat. The bacteria spreads through airborne droplets and shared personal items. *C. diphtheriae* creates a toxin in the body that produces a thick, gray or black coating in the nose, throat, or airway, which can also affect the heart and nervous system. Even with proper antibiotic treatment, diphtheria kills about 10 percent of the people who contract it. The first diphtheria vaccine was unveiled in 1913, and although vaccination has made a major dent in mortality rates, the disease still exists in developing countries and other areas where people are not regularly vaccinated. The World Health Organization (WHO) estimates that worldwide there are about 5,000 deaths from diphtheria annually, but the disease is quite rare in the United States, with fewer than five cases reported each year.

3. Invasive H. Flu: Invasive H. flu, or Hib disease, is an infection caused by the *Haemophilus influenzae* type b (Hib) bacteria, which spreads when an infected person coughs, sneezes, or speaks. Invasive H. flu is a bit of a misnomer because it is not related to any form of the influenza virus. However, it can lead to bacterial meningitis (a potentially fatal brain infection), pneumonia, epiglottitis (severe swelling above the voice box that makes breathing difficult), and infections of the blood, joints, bones, and pericardium (the covering of the heart).

Children younger than five years old are particularly susceptible to the Hib bacteria because they have not had the chance to develop immunity to it. The first Hib vaccine was licensed in 1985, but despite its success in the developed world, the disease is still prevalent in the developing countries. WHO estimates that each year Hib disease causes two to three million cases of serious illness worldwide, mostly pneumonia and meningitis, and 450,000 deaths of young children.

4. Malaria: This disease is a parasitic infection of the liver and red blood cells. In its mildest forms it can produce flu-like symptoms and nausea, and in its severest forms it can cause seizures, coma, fluid buildup in the lungs, kidney failure, and death. Female mosquitoes of the genus *Anopheles* transmit the disease. When the mosquito bites, the parasites enter a person's body, invading red blood cells and causing the cells to rupture. As the cells burst, they release chemicals that cause malaria's symptoms. About 350 million to 500 million cases of malaria occur worldwide every year. About one million are fatal, with children in sub-Saharan Africa accounting for most of the deaths. Other high-risk areas include Central and South America, India, and the Middle East. Malaria is treated with a variety of drugs, some of which kill the parasites once they're in the blood and others that prevent infection in the first place. Of course, if you can avoid the parasite-carrying mosquitoes, you can avoid malaria, so the disease is often controlled using mosquito repellent and bed netting, especially in poor countries that cannot afford medications.

5. Measles: Measles is a highly contagious viral illness of the respiratory system that spreads through airborne droplets when an infected person coughs or sneezes. Although the first symptoms of measles mimic a simple cold, with a cough, runny nose, and red watery eyes, this disease is more serious. As measles progresses, the infected person develops a fever and a red or brownish-red skin rash. Complications can include diarrhea, pneumonia, brain infection, and even death, although these are seen more commonly in malnourished or immunodeficient people. Measles has historically been a devastating disease, but measles vaccination prevented an estimated 21.1 million deaths between 2000 and 2017. Until 1963, when the first measles vaccine was used in the United States, almost everyone got the measles by age 20. There has been a 99 percent reduction in measles since then, but outbreaks have occurred when the disease is brought over from other countries or when children don't get the vaccine or all the required doses. Most children today receive the measles vaccine as part of the MMR vaccination, which protects against measles, mumps, and rubella (German measles).

6. Pertussis: Whoop, there it is—and if you suspect someone has it, move away. Pertussis, or whooping cough, is a highly contagious respiratory infection caused by the *Bordetella pertussis* bacteria. The descriptive nickname comes from the "whooping" sounds that infected children make after one of the disease's coughing spells. The coughing fits spread the bacteria and can last a minute or longer, causing a child to turn purple or red and sometimes vomit. Severe episodes can cause a lack of oxygen to the brain. Adults who contract pertussis usually have a hacking cough rather than a whooping one. Although the disease can strike anyone, it is most prevalent in infants under age one because they haven't received the entire course of pertussis vaccinations. The pertussis vaccine was first used in 1933, but adolescents and adults become susceptible when the immunity from childhood vaccinations wanes and they don't get booster shots. According to the CDC, pertussis causes 10 to 20 deaths each year in the United States, and there were more than 18,900 cases reported in the U.S. in 2017. Worldwide, the disease causes far more damage—about 24.1 million people are infected annually, and the CDC estimates around 160,700 deaths each year.

7. Pneumococcal Disease: Pneumococcal disease is the collective name for the infections caused by *Streptococcus pneumoniae* bacteria, also known as *pneumococcus*. This bacteria finds a home all over the body. The most common types of infections caused by *S. pneumoniae* are middle ear infections, pneumonia, bacteremia (bloodstream infections), sinus infections, and bacterial meningitis. There are more than 90 types of pneumococcus, with the ten most common types responsible for 62 percent of the world's invasive diseases. Those infected carry the bacteria in their throats and expel it when they cough or sneeze. Like any other germ, *S. pneumoniae* can infect anyone, but certain population groups are more at risk, such as the elderly, people with cancer or AIDS, and people with a chronic illness such as diabetes. The CDC blames pneumococcal disease for the deaths of 200 children under the age of five each year in the United States. WHO estimates that annually pneumococcal disease is responsible for one million fatal cases of respiratory illness alone; most of these cases occur in developing countries. There are two types of vaccines available to prevent pneumococcal disease, which the CDC recommends that children and adults older than age 65 receive.

8. Polio: Of the deadly infectious diseases for which science has developed vaccines and treatments, people are most familiar with the victory over polio. The disease is caused by a virus that enters the body through the mouth, usually from hands contaminated with the stool of an infected person. In about 95 percent of cases, polio produces no symptoms at all (asymptomatic polio), but in the remaining cases of polio, the disease can take three forms. Abortive polio creates flu-like symptoms, such as upper respiratory infection, fever, sore throat, and general malaise. Nonparalytic polio is more severe and produces symptoms similar to mild meningitis, including sensitivity to light and neck stiffness. Finally, paralytic polio produces the symptoms with which most people associate the disease, even though paralytic polio accounts for less than 1 percent of all cases. Paralytic polio causes loss of control and paralysis of limbs, reflexes, and the muscles that control breathing. Today, polio is under control in the developed world, and world health authorities are close to controlling the disease in developing countries, as well. Dr. Jonas Salk's inactivated polio vaccine (IPV) first appeared in 1955, and Dr. Albert Sabin's oral polio vaccine (OPV) first appeared in 1961. Children in the United States receive IPV, but most children in developing areas of the world receive OPV, which is cheaper and doesn't have to be administered by a health-care professional; however, in rare instances, OPV can cause polio.

9. Tetanus: Reproductive cells (spores) of *Clostridium tetani* are found in the soil and enter the body through a skin wound. Once the spores develop into mature bacteria, the bacteria produce tetanospasmin, a neurotoxin (a protein that poisons the body's nervous system) that causes muscle spasms. In fact, tetanus gets its nickname—lockjaw—because the toxin often attacks the muscles that control the jaw. Lockjaw is accompanied by difficulty swallowing and painful stiffness in the neck, shoulders, and back. The spasms can then spread to the muscles of the abdomen, upper arms, and thighs. According to the CDC, tetanus is fatal in about 11 percent of cases, but fortunately, it can't be spread from person to person—you need direct contact with *C. tetani* to contract the disease. Today, tetanus immunization is standard in the United States, but if you are injured in a way that increases tetanus risk (i.e. stepping on a rusty nail, cutting your hand with a knife, or getting bitten by a dog), a booster shot may be necessary if it's been several years since your last tetanus shot. According to the CDC, since the 1970s, only about 50 to 100 cases of tetanus are reported in the United States each year, mostly among people who have never been vaccinated or who did not get a booster shot. And WHO says that globally there were 12,476 reported cases of tetanus in 2017.

10. Typhoid Fever: Typhoid is usually spread when food or water has been infected with *Salmonella typhi*, most often through contact with the feces of an infected person. Once the typhoid bacteria enter the bloodstream, the body mounts a defense that causes a high fever, headache, stomach pains, weakness, and decreased appetite. Occasionally, people who have typhoid get a rash of flat red spots. Because sewage treatment in the United States is quite good, the disease is very rare, and the CDC reports only about 400 cases of it annually. However, people who live in developing countries where there is little water and sewage treatment, or where hand washing is not a common practice, are at high risk. Prime typhoid fever areas are in Africa, Asia, the Caribbean, India, and Central and South America. WHO estimates 11 to 21 million cases occur globally with 128,000 to 161,000 typhoid-related deaths each year. Despite these daunting statistics, typhoid fever vaccination is available for people who travel to high-risk areas, and the disease can be effectively treated with antibiotics. Without treatment, the fever can continue for weeks or months, and the infection can lead to death.

11. Yellow Fever: Yellow fever is spread by mosquitoes infected with the yellow fever virus. Jaundice, or yellowing of the skin and eyes, is the hallmark of the infection and gives it its name. Most cases of yellow fever are mild and require only three or four days to recover, but severe cases can cause bleeding, heart problems, liver or kidney failure, brain dysfunction, or death. People with the disease can ease their symptoms, but there is no specific treatment, so prevention via the yellow fever vaccine is key. The vaccine provides lifelong protection against the disease and is generally safe for everyone older than nine months. Yellow fever occurs only in Africa, South America, and some areas of the Caribbean, so only travelers who are destined for these regions need to be concerned about it. WHO estimates that yellow fever causes 200,000 cases of the disease and 30,000 deaths each year. The elderly are at highest risk of developing the most severe symptoms. Vaccination and mosquito-eradication efforts have made a great difference.

12. Smallpox: Unlike other diseases on this list, which can still appear in outbreaks when vaccination vigilance weakens, smallpox has been wiped off the face of the earth, except for samples of the virus held in labs for research purposes. Symptoms of smallpox included a high fever, head and body aches, malaise, vomiting, and a rash of small red bumps that progressed into sores that could break open and spread the virus (the virus could also be spread via contact with shared items, clothing, and bedding). Smallpox was an entirely human disease—it did not infect any other animal or insect on the planet. Thus, once vaccination eliminated the chances of the virus spreading among the human population, the disease disappeared; in fact, the United States has not vaccinated for smallpox since 1972. Although smallpox was one of the most devastating illnesses in human history, killing more than 300 million people worldwide during the 20th century alone, scientists declared the world free of smallpox in 1979. The naturally occurring disease has been eradicated, but fears remain about the smallpox samples being used as bioweapons.

Early Contraception

Ever since humans realized how babies were made, they have tried to control the process. In earlier days, some techniques were more successful than others.

An ancient Greek gynecologist told women not wishing to have a child to jump backward seven times after intercourse. Ancient Roman women tried to avoid pregnancy by tying a pouch containing a cat's liver to their left foot or by spitting into the mouth of a frog.

Barrier methods of contraception have included pebbles, half a lemon, and dried elephant or crocodile dung. In 1550 B.C., a suggested concoction of ground dates, acacia tree bark, and honey applied locally was probably fairly effective, since acacia ferments into lactic acid, which disrupts a normal pH balance. In eastern Canada, one aboriginal group believed in the efficacy of women drinking a tea brewed with beaver testicles.

As early as the seventh century B.C., a member of the fennel family called silphium was discovered to be an extremely effective "morning-after pill." But since it only grew in a small area on the Libyan mountainside and attempts to cultivate it elsewhere failed, silphium was extinct by the second century.

Men have almost always used some sort of sheath, dating back to at least 1000 B.C. The ancient Romans and the 17th-century British employed animal intestine, while the Egyptians and Italians preferred fabric, which they sometimes soaked in a spermicidal solution. Vulcanized rubber appeared around 1844.

Rasputin: Gifted Healer or Depraved Charlatan?

We know this much: Rasputin, a barely literate Russian peasant, grew close to the last tsaritsa—close enough to cost him his life. Incredibly lurid stories ricocheted off the walls of the Winter Palace: drunken satyr, faith healer, master manipulator. What's true? And why does Rasputin continue to fascinate us to this very day?

On January 22, 1869, Grigory Yefimovich Rasputin was born in the peasant village of Pokrovskoe, Russia. Baby Rasputin entered the world on the day of the Orthodox saint Grigory and was named after him. There wasn't much to distinguish little Grigory from tens of millions of Russian peasant kids, and he grew into a rowdy drunk. He married a fellow peasant named Praskovia, who hung back in Pokrovskoe raising their three kids in Rasputin's general absence.

At 28, Rasputin was born again, rural Russian style. He sobered up and wandered between monasteries seeking knowledge. Evidently, he fell in with the *khlysti*—a secretive, heretical Eastern Orthodox sect swirling with rumors of orgies, flagellation, and the like. Rasputin gained a mystical aura during this time.

In 1903, he wandered to the capital, St. Petersburg, where he impressed the local Orthodox clergy. Word

spread. The ruling Romanov family soon heard of Rasputin.

The Romanovs held a powerful yet precarious position. Ethnically, they were more German than Russian, a hot-button topic for the Slavs they ruled over. Greedy flatterers and brutal infighters made the corridors of power a steep slope with weak rock and loose mud: As you climbed, your prestige and influence grew—but woe to you if you slipped (or were pushed). In that event, the rest would step aside and let you fall—caring only to get out of your way. This was no safe place for a naive peasant, however spiritually inclined. Even the Romanovs lived in fear, for tsars tended to die violent deaths. They ruled a dirt-poor population seething with resentment. Tsaryevich ("tsar's son") Alexei, the heir apparent, was a fragile hemophiliac who could bleed out from a skinned knee, aptly symbolic of the blood in the political water in St. Petersburg in those final days of the last tsar, Nicholas II.

RASPUTIN FINDS A FRIEND IN THE TSARITSA

As the tsaritsa worried over gravely ill Alexei in 1906, she thought of Rasputin and his healing reputation. He answered her summons in person, blessed Alexei with an Orthodox *ikon*, and left. Alexei improved, and Tsaritsa Alexandra was hooked on Rasputin. She consulted him often, introduced him to her friends, and pulled him onto that treacherous slope of imperial favor. Rasputin became a polarizing figure as he grew more influential. His small covey of upper-crust supporters (who were mostly female) hung on his every word, even as a growing legion of nobles, peasants, and clergy saw Rasputin as emblematic of all that was wrong with the monarchy.

What few ask now is: What was Rasputin thinking? What was he feeling? His swift rise from muddy fields to the royal palace gave him an understandable ego trip. He was not an idiot; he surely realized his rise would earn him jealous enemies. The sheer fury of their hatred seems to have surprised, frightened, and saddened him, for he wasn't a hateful man. He certainly felt duty-bound to the tsaritsa, whose unwavering favor deflected most of his enemies' blows. Rasputin's internal spiritual struggle between sinfulness and holiness registers authentic, though it is an established fact that he made regular visits to prostitutes. Defenders claim that he was only steeling himself against sexual temptation; one can imagine what his enemies said.

Life worsened for Rasputin in 1914, when he was stabbed by a former prostitute. After recuperating, he abandoned any restraint he'd ever exercised. Rasputin began drinking again and had many and varied sexual encounters; perhaps he expected death and gave in to his desires. After Russia went to war with Germany, cartoons portrayed Rasputin as a cancer infecting the monarchy. Military setbacks left Russians with much to mourn and resent. A wave of mandatory patriotism swept Russia, focusing discontent upon the royal family's Germanic ties.

In the end, clergy and nobility agreed with the media: down with Rasputin.

A VIOLENT DEMISE

Led by a fabulously rich libertine named Felix Yusupov, Rasputin's enemies lured him to a meeting on December 29, 1916. The popular story is that he scarfed a bunch of poisoned food and wine, somehow didn't die, was shot, got up, was beaten and shot some more, then was finally tied up and thrown into an icy river. What is sure: Rasputin was shot, bound, and dumped into freezing water to die.

The tsaritsa buried her advisor on royal property. After the Romanovs fell, a mob dug up Rasputin and burned his corpse. Nothing remains of him.

Rasputin had predicted that if he were slain by the nobility, the Russian monarchy wouldn't long survive him. His prophecy came true: Less than a year after his death, the Russian Revolution deposed the tsar. The Bolsheviks would soon murder the entire royal family; had they captured Rasputin, it's hard to imagine him being spared. For the "Mad Monk" who was neither mad nor monastic, the muddy road of life had dead-ended in the treacherous forest of imperial favor.

History's Grim Places of Quarantine

Life has never been easy for lepers. Throughout history, they've been stigmatized, feared, and cast out by society. Such reactions—though undeniably heartless—were perhaps understandable because the disease was thought to be rampantly contagious. Anyone suspected of leprosy was forced into quarantine and left to die.

Leprosy has affected humanity since at least 600 B.C. This condition, which is now called Hansen's disease, attacks the nervous system primarily in the hands, feet, and face. It causes disfiguring skin sores, nerve damage, and progressive debilitation. Medical science had no understanding of the condition until the late 1800s and no effective treatment for it until the 1940s. Prior to that point, patients faced a slow, painful, and certain demise.

Misinterpretations of the Bible passage Leviticus 13:45–46, which labeled lepers as "unclean" and dictated that sufferers must "dwell apart . . . outside the camp," didn't help matters. (The "leprosy" cited in Leviticus referred to several skin conditions, but Hansen's disease was not one of them.) It's really no surprise that society's less-than-compassionate response to the disease was the leper colony.

The first leper colonies were isolated spots in the wilderness where the afflicted were driven, forgotten, and left to die.

The practice of exiling lepers continued well into the 20th century. In Crete, for instance, lepers were banished to mountainside caves, where they survived by eating scraps left by wolves. More humane measures were adopted in 1903, when lepers were corralled into the Spinalonga Island leper colony and given food and shelter and cared for by priests and nuns. However, once you entered, you never left, and it remained that way until the colony's last resident died in 1957.

Still, joining a leper colony sometimes beat living among the healthy. It wasn't much fun wandering from town to town while wearing signs or ringing bells to warn of one's affliction. And you were always susceptible to violence from townsfolk gripped by irrational fear—as when lepers were blamed for epidemic outbreaks and thrown into bonfires as punishment.

LIFE IN THE AMERICAN COLONY

American attitudes toward lepers weren't any more enlightened. One of modernity's most notorious leper colonies was on the Hawaiian island of Molokai. It was established in 1866.

Hawaiian kings and American officials banished sufferers to this remote peninsula ringed by jagged lava rock and towering sea cliffs. Molokai became one of the world's largest leper colonies—its population peaked in 1890 at 1,174—and more than 8,000 people were forcibly confined there before the practice was finally ended in 1969.

The early days of Molokai were horrible. The banished were abandoned in a lawless place where they received minimal care and had to fight with others for food, water, blankets, and shelter. Public condemnation and the efforts of such caring individuals as Father Damien de Veuster led to improved conditions on Molokai. The practice of sending the afflicted to Molokai ended in 1969; some individuals remain, however, because it is where they feel most at home.

A LEPER HAVEN IN LOUISIANA

While sufferers of leprosy were being humiliated in Hawaii, they were being helped in Louisiana.

In 1894, the Louisiana Leper House, which billed itself as "a place of treatment and research, not detention," opened in Carville. In 1920, it was transferred to federal authority and renamed the National Leprosarium of the United States. Known today as the National Hansen's Disease (leprosy) Program (NHDP), the facility became a leading research and rehabilitation center, pioneering treatments that form the basis of multidrug therapies currently prescribed by the World Health Organization (WHO) for the treatment of Hansen's disease.

It was here that researchers enlisted a common Louisiana critter—the armadillo—in the fight against the disease. It had always been difficult to study Hansen's disease. Human nerves are seldom biopsied, so direct data on nerve damage from Hansen's was minimal.

But in the 1960s, NHDP researchers theorized that armadillos might be susceptible to the germ because of their low body temperature. They began inoculating armadillos with it and discovered that the animals could develop the disease systemically. Now the armadillo is used to develop infected nerves for research worldwide.

A THING OF THE PAST?

In 1985, Hansen's disease was still considered a public health problem in 122 countries. In fact, the last remaining leper colony, located in Croatia, didn't close until 2002. However, WHO has made great strides toward eradicating the disease; by 2000, the rate of infection had dropped by 90 percent. The multidrug therapies currently prescribed for the treatment of Hansen's disease are available to all patients for free via WHO. In the last two decades, approximately 16 million patients have been cured.

Bathing Is Bad for You—Huh?

As late as 1920, barely one out of a hundred American homes had bathtubs. The lack of bathing facilities wasn't due to inferior technology or inadequate sanitation, but to prevailing attitudes. From the time of the Renaissance, most Europeans were wary of bathing—deeming it unhealthy.

The terrible plagues of the late Middle Ages may have contributed to hydrophobia. Diseases such as cholera and typhoid were spread by filthy water. The people of the time didn't know about germs but may have intuited the link between bad water and ill health. The phrase "catch your death of cold" arose during an era when there was no hot running water.

By the time of America's colonization, the fear of water had taken firm root. When John Smith and his fellow settlers moved to Jamestown, Virginia, the native Powhatans, who bathed every day, literally held their noses when downwind of the colonists.

But it wasn't always so.

LIGHT IN DARKNESS

Contrary to myth, folks in the "Dark Ages" were relatively enlightened about cleanliness. According to the book *A History of Private Life*, medieval fabliaux—tall tales like those of Chaucer—are replete with lovers taking hot baths before love-making. Ladies and lords of the manor soaked on stools placed in wooden vats filled with hot water. They also scrubbed their hands and faces before meals and washed their mouths out after, according to the etiquette guides of the time. The more common folk soaked in urban public baths called "stews," the opening of which were heralded by the sound of trumpet and drum each morning. Doughty burghers marched to the stews naked to stop thieves from picking their pockets. Inside, the two sexes bathed together, sometimes clothed.

The Catholic Church frowned on the mixed-gender aspect. Some orders of monks prescribed bathing only for Christmas and Easter, with the private parts covered during these sacred ablutions. But the clergy wasn't totally doctrinaire. The founder of the modern papacy, Pope Gregory I, advised taking a bath each Sunday. And monasteries featured *lavabos*, fountains for hand washing.

Hildegard of Bingen (1098–1179), a noted early scientist, offered these prescriptions for good health: "If a person's head has an ailment, it should be washed frequently in this water and it will be healed . . . If your lord wishes to bathe and wash his body clean . . . have a basin full of hot fresh herbs and wash his body with a soft sponge." Along with roses, herbs added to bath water included hollyhock, brown fennel, danewort, chamomile, and green oats. (At times, the Middle Ages sound positively New Age.)

Hildegard also offered advice for overly randy fellows: "A man who has an overabundance in his loins should cook wild lettuce in water and pour that water over himself in a sauna bath."

BATHING'S BAD RAP

By the 1400s, however, public opinion had swung the other way. Fires were common in the public baths, where water was heated by the burning of wood. Wood itself was hard to find as growing prosperity led to the leveling of forests. Moreover, peasants often fell ill from the custom of the entire family washing from the same barrel of water.

Furthermore, it was believed that disease spread by way of vapors that passed into the skin through pores that opened during bathing. (This is where the term *malaria*, which means "bad air," comes from.) No less an authority than English philosopher Francis Bacon advised: "After Bathing, wrap the Body in a seare-cloth made of Masticke, Myrrh, Pomander, and Saffron, for staying the perspiration or breathing of the pores." If body odor

lingered, courtiers—male and female—cloaked their smell with copious applications of cologne.

Yet, attitudes were never monolithic. In the spring of 1511, the diary of one Lucas Rem of Germany reports that he took 127 baths. Thinking was slowly turning back in the direction of sanitary health.

BACK TO CLEANLINESS

In the mid-19th century, bathing bounced back in the United States. Millions of the "unwashed masses" were forsaking farms for crowded, filthy cities, and millions more were arriving on immigrant ships. In response, the healthier, better-educated natives crusaded for better health. Healthy living—physical and spiritual—became all the rage.

One fad among the wealthy was "taking the waters" at spas such as Saratoga Springs, New York, which was frequented by Edgar Allan Poe and Franklin Roosevelt.

In the 1880s, the Standard Sanitary Manufacturing Company made cast-iron bathtubs available to the public. These were actually advertised as horse troughs/bathtubs; few thought anyone would buy a tub only for bathing.

During the Roaring Twenties, middle-class folk, envious of mansions trendily outfitted with indoor plumbing, began putting sinks, toilets, and tubs into separate rooms called bathrooms.

Today, Americans are famous the world over for their frequent showering. Sir John Harington, inventor of the water closet, would be pleased.

CHAPTER 9

THE ART OF IT ALL

Cracking the Code of da Vinci's Masterpiece

After centuries of beguiling viewers—and maddening artists and scientists who tried to uncover its secrets—Leonardo da Vinci's *Mona Lisa* may have finally revealed her secret code.

The Renaissance genius began his portrait of Lisa del Giocondo, a Florentine gentlewoman, in 1503 and is believed to have finished the painting just before his death in 1519. Using a process of brushwork he called "sfumato" (from the Italian *fumo*, meaning smoke), Leonardo created a painting that he said was composed "without lines or borders, in the manner of smoke or beyond the focus plane." Although he left many notes on his other projects, Leonardo never explained how he created the subtle effects of light and shadow that give his masterwork its realistic, three-dimensional quality.

Although the painting has been studied extensively over the centuries, even the most modern scientific instruments have been unable to uncover all of its secrets.

French artist and art historian Jacques Franck, however, believes he has discovered Leonardo's methods through his own trial and error. According to Franck, after completing a conventional sketch of his subject, Leonardo applied a base coat of pale yellow imprimatura—a diluted semiopaque wash—then began one of history's greatest creative marathons. Using minute crosshatching techniques, Leonardo spent more than 15 years brushing on 30 successive layers of paint. Apparently requiring a magnifying glass, the process took 30 to 40 small dots of oil paint smaller than the head of a pin to cover one square millimeter of canvas. Franck believes Leonardo applied additional layers of imprimatura between each layer of paint to further soften lines and blend colors, creating successively finer layers of shading and tones.

Although Franck's conclusions have been disputed by some art historians, he has convincingly reproduced the effects with his own copies of small sections of the painting. An exhibit at the Uffizi Gallery in Florence displayed six panels by Franck that re-create one of the eyes from the *Mona Lisa* and illustrate the step-by-step process of how Leonardo may have worked.

Though his artistic sleuthing remains controversial, Franck points out that the use of minute dots of paint—similar to the pointillism developed by modern artists—

is an artistic technique that has been used since Roman times and is clearly evident in some of Leonardo's earlier paintings. With the *Mona Lisa*, Leonardo apparently took the technique to an unmatched level.

Other research has used a noninvasive technique called x-ray fluorescence spectroscopy to study the layers and chemical compositions of Leonardo's works. These studies have revealed that he was constantly testing new methods. He did not always use glaze, for example, and while working on the *Mona Lisa*, he mixed manganese oxide in with his paint. Ongoing studies are sure to reveal even more of da Vinci's masterful techniques.

The Louvre: Gift of the Revolution

Built by French kings over six centuries, the famed Louvre found its true calling with the bloody end of the dynasty that built it.

The art collection known throughout the world as the Louvre began as a moated, medieval arsenal erected to protect the city's inhabitants against the Anglo-Norman threat. Built by King Philippe Auguste in the late 12th century, the fortress lost much of its military value as the city expanded far beyond the castle walls over the next 150 years. In 1364, King Charles V had the Louvre redesigned as a royal residence.

During the next three centuries, French kings and queens remodeled and redesigned portions of the Louvre, connecting it with the nearby Tuileries palace. Apartments and galleries were added, and remnants of the medieval fortress were demolished.

During the reign of King Louis XIV, the palace came into its own, as classical paintings and sculptures by the great artists of the day graced the palace's walls and ceilings. Work halted briefly in 1672, when Louis moved the French court to his fantastic palace at Versailles, but in 1692 Louis sent a set of antique sculptures back to the Louvre's Salle de Caryatides, inaugurating the first of the Louvre's many antique accessions. Academies of arts and sciences took up residence at the palace, and in 1699, the Académie Royale de Peinture et de Sculpture held its first exhibition in the Louvre's Grand Galerie.

The artistic treasures housed by the French monarchs were, of course, the property of the king and off-limits to the masses. But in 1791, in the wake of the French Revolution, the French Assemblée Nationale declared all Bourbon property to be held by the state for the people of France. The government established a public art and science museum at the Louvre and Tuileries, and in 1793, the year King Louis XVI and his queen, Marie Antoinette, were sent to the guillotine, the Museum Central des Arts opened its doors to the public.

As Napoleon's armies marched through Italy, Austria, and Egypt in the late 1790s, the museum's collections grew with the spoils of war. Napoleon and Empress Josephine inaugurated an antiquities gallery at the Louvre in 1800, and three years later, the museum was briefly renamed the Musée Napoléon. With the emperor's fall in 1815, however, the Louvre's status diminished as many of its artifacts were returned to their rightful owners.

A REPRESENTATIVE COLLECTION

In the mid-19th century, the Louvre opened additional galleries to showcase Spanish, Algerian, and Egyptian art. As the Louvre soldiered on into the 20th century, its more exotic holdings—particularly Islamic and Middle Eastern art—expanded, and the museum was progressively remodeled to accommodate its growing collection.

At the outbreak of World War II, French officials fretted that the Louvre's holdings would become a target for Nazi pillage, so they dispersed most of the treasures among the Loire valley chateaus. The Nazis had the museum reopened in September 1940, though there was little left for the cowed Parisians to view until the country was liberated four years later.

In 1945, the restored French government reorganized its national art collections, and in 1983 the government announced a sweeping reorganization and remodeling plan under the direction of the famed Chinese American architect I. M. Pei. Impressionist and other late 19th-century works were moved to the Musée d'Orsay, while Pei's famous glass pyramid, which towers over the Cour Napoleon, signaled a new stage in the Louvre's life. Further renovations from 1993 to the present have given the Louvre its distinctive look, as well as its status as one of the world's premier museums.

The First American Novel

Steeped in controversy, the plot of the first American novel—with its themes of seduction, incest, and suicide—would be more readily accepted in today's culture than it was in late 18th-century America.

William Hill Brown wrote *The Power of Sympathy*, the first American novel, in 1789. Printer Isaiah Thomas was contracted to publish a limited run of the book and to sell it through his two bookshops. In an ironic twist—given the historical significance the book later assumed—*The Power of Sympathy* was presented as the work of an anonymous author.

Even if the book had been properly credited at the outset, few readers outside of upper-crust Boston would have been familiar with the author. When *The Power of Sympathy* appeared, William Hill Brown was a reasonably prolific but little-known playwright; he later wrote a comic opera, poetry, essays, and two more novels.

The son of a respected clockmaker, Brown was born in Boston in November 1765. He attended the Boston

Boy's School, where he pursued creative writing, a craft encouraged by his step-aunt. Brown spent his formative years in an upper-class Boston neighborhood, living across the street from a married, politically active lawyer named Perez Morton.

In 1788, rumors of a romantic scandal involving Morton and his sister-in-law, Frances Apthorp, circulated among Boston's elite. The rumor turned out to be true, and rather than face public ridicule, the mortified Frances committed suicide. Perez, on the other hand, continued with his life as though nothing had happened. The public apparently went along with this tactic; Morton was later elected speaker of the lower house in the General Court of Massachusetts in 1806 and was named attorney general in 1810.

Writer (and former neighbor) William Brown was naturally well aware of the Morton-Apthorp scandal and published his book just a year later.

Following a novelistic style popular during the period, *The Power of Sympathy* unfolds via letters exchanged by central and secondary characters. The stinger is that the protagonists, Thomas Harrington and Harriot Fawcett, are about to unknowingly embark on an incestuous relationship.

In the novel, Harriot is Thomas's half-sister, born out of wedlock to a mistress of Thomas's father. For obvious reasons of propriety, the pregnancy and birth had been kept secret from the community and the rest of the family. When Harriot discovers the truth, she commits suicide. The facts soon become clear to Thomas as well, and he elects to follow his half-sister in suicide.

CREDIT WHERE CREDIT IS DUE

Pressure from the Morton and Apthorp families, as well as from other prominent citizens, forced Brown to remove his book from circulation. Many copies were subsequently destroyed, and few exist today. In an odd twist, when the novel was reissued in the 19th century—nearly 100 years later—it was attributed to a deceased, once-popular Boston poet named Sarah Apthorp Morton, who happened to be the wife of Perez Morton—the man whose indiscretion helped inspire the novel in the first place! A correction issued by William Brown's aged niece not long after the book's republication led to proper attribution at last. Brown would finally be recognized as the author of the first novel written and published in America.

Art on Trial

The publication of Gustave Flaubert's *Madame Bovary* shocked national sensibility and caused Flaubert to be charged with offending morality and religion.

THE CASE

When *Madame Bovary* was first published serially in the *Revue de Paris* in 1851, the *Revue*'s editor, Leon Laurent-Pichat; the work's author, Gustave Flaubert; and the publisher, Auguste-Alexis Pillet, were charged with "offenses to public morality and religion" by the conservative Restoration Government of Napoleon III. Many, including Flaubert, believed that his work was being singled out because of the regime's distaste for the notoriously liberal *Revue*.

Prosecutor Ernest Pinard based his case upon the premise that adultery must always be condemned as an affront to the sanctity of marriage and society at large. In this, Pinard had a point. The novel conspicuously lacks any voice reminding the reader that adultery is reprehensible and simply tells the tale of Emma Bovary's gradual but inevitable acceptance of her need for sexual satisfaction outside the confines of a provincial marriage. Other works of the period, notably the popular plays of Alexandre Dumas, commonly featured adulterous characters. But in these, there was a voice of reason reminding the audience that the character's actions were wrong. That *Madame Bovary* lacked such perspective was certainly unprecedented and—according to the government—worthy of censure.

THE DEFENSE

Defense attorney Jules Sénard (a close friend of Flaubert's and one of the people to whom the work was dedicated) argued that literature must always be considered art for art's sake and that Flaubert was a consummate artist whose intentions had nothing to do with affecting society at large.

Whether or not Flaubert intended to undermine any aspect of French society is debatable. The son in a wealthy family, he could afford to sit in his ivory tower and decry what he perceived as the petty hypocrisies of the emerging middle class. Certainly, Gustave Flaubert was a perfectionist who spent weeks reworking single pages of prose. In *Madame Bovary*, he sought to create a novel that was stylistically beautiful. To test his craft, Flaubert would shout passages out loud to test their rhythm. It took the author five years of solitary toil to complete the work. The literary elite, notably Sainte-Beuve, Victor Hugo, and Charles-Pierre Baudelaire, immediately recognized the novel's genius, but the general public largely ignored the work when it was first published.

THE VERDICT

In the end, the judges agreed with Sénard and acquitted all of the accused—but not before the sensational trial had sparked public interest in a work that might otherwise have gone unnoticed by the very society (the emerging middle class) the trial was meant to protect.

The Mysterious Voynich Manuscript

Dubbed the "World's Most Mysterious Book," the Voynich manuscript contains more than 200 vellum pages of vivid, colorful illustrations and handwritten prose. There's only one small problem: No one knows what any of it means—or whether it means anything at all.

It was "discovered" in 1912 after being hidden from the world for almost 250 years. An American antique book dealer named Wilfried Voynich came across the medieval manuscript at an Italian Jesuit College. Approximately nine inches by six inches in size, the manuscript bore a soft, light-brown vellum cover, which was unmarked, untitled, and gave no indication as to when it had been written or by whom.

Bound inside were approximately 230 yellow parchment pages, most of which contained richly colored drawings of strange plants, celestial bodies, and other scientific matter. Many of the pages were adorned by naked nymphs bathing in personal-size washtubs. Handwritten text in flowing script accompanied the illustrations.

Although Voynich was an expert antiquarian, he was baffled by the book's contents. And today—nearly a century later—the manuscript that came to bear his name remains a mystery.

WEIRD SCIENCE

The mystery surrounding the Voynich manuscript begins with its content, which reads (so to speak) like a work of weird science presented in six identifiable "sections":

◆ a botanical section, containing drawings of plants that no botanist has ever been able to identify

◆ an astronomical section, with illustrations of the sun, moon, stars, and zodiac symbols surrounded by the ever-present bathing nymphs

◆ a "biological" section, showing perplexing anatomical drawings of chambers or organs connected by tubes—and which also features more nymphs swimming in their inner liquids

◆ a cosmological section, consisting mostly of unexplained circular drawings

◆ a pharmaceutical section, depicting drawings of plant parts (leaves, roots) placed next to containers

◆ a recipe section, featuring short paragraphs "bulleted" by stars in the margin

Weirder still are the ubiquitous nymphs—a nice touch perhaps, but how they relate to the subject matter is anyone's guess.

MANY MYSTERIES, STILL NO ANSWERS

And then there's the enigmatic text. The world's greatest cryptologists have failed to unravel its meaning. Even the American and British code breakers who cracked the Japanese and German codes in World War II were stumped. To this day, not a single word of the Voynich manuscript has been deciphered.

This, of course, has led to key unsolved questions, namely:

◆ Who wrote it? A letter found with the manuscript,

dated 1666, credits Roger Bacon, a Franciscan friar who lived from 1214 to 1294. This has since been discredited because the manuscript's date of origin is generally considered to be between 1450 and 1500. There are as many theories about who wrote it as there are nymphs among its pages. In fact, some believe Voynich forged the whole thing.

❖ What is it? It was first thought to be a coded description of Bacon's early scientific discoveries. Since then, other theories ranging from an ancient prayer book written in a pidgin Germanic language to one big, elaborate hoax (aside from that supposedly perpetrated by Voynich) have been posited.

❖ Is it real writing? Is the script composed in a variation of a known language, a lost language, an encrypted language, an artificial language? Or is it just plain gibberish?

WHAT DO WE KNOW?

Despite the aura of mystery surrounding the manuscript, it has been possible to trace its travels over the past 400 years. The earliest known owner was Holy Roman Emperor Rudolph II, who purchased it in 1586. By 1666, the manuscript had passed through a series of owners to Athanasius Kircher, a Jesuit scholar who hid it in the college where Voynich found it 250 years later.

After being passed down to various members of Voynich's estate, the manuscript was sold in 1961 to a rare-book collector who sought to resell it for a fortune. After failing to find a buyer, he donated it to Yale University, where it currently resides—still shrouded in mystery—in the Beinecke Rare Book and Manuscript Library.

To this day, efforts to translate the Voynich manuscript continue. And still, the manuscript refuses to yield its secrets, leading experts to conclude that it's either an ingenious hoax or the ultimate unbreakable code.

The hoax theory gained some ground in 2004 when Dr. Gordon Rugg, a computer-science lecturer at Keele University, announced that he had replicated the Voynich manuscript using a low-tech device called a Cardan grille. According to Rugg, this proved that the manuscript was likely a fraud—a volume of gibberish created, perhaps, by the infamous Edward Kelley in an attempt to con money out of Emperor Rudolph II.

Mystery solved? Well, it's not quite that simple. Many researchers remain unconvinced. Sure, Rugg demonstrated that the manuscript might be a hoax. But the possibility that it is not a hoax remains. And thus, the search for meaning continues . . .

God's Architect

More than 90 years after his death, Antoni Gaudí's greatest work is still under construction.

Antoni Gaudí was born in Catalan, Spain, in 1852. As a boy, he was fascinated by the shapes peculiar to the natural environment of his boyhood home—a lifelong inspiration that would later take form in the fantastical designs of his buildings.

After studying architecture in Barcelona in the 1870s, he began work on a series of commissions for private homes and commercial buildings, some of which stand as the most innovative architecture ever built.

In 1883, Gaudí accepted a commission to build a new church in the heart of Barcelona. Inspired by the strange mountains at nearby Montserrat, his design for La Sagrada Família (Holy Family Church) called for 18 towers more than 300 feet tall, with a 580-foot-tall central tower representing Jesus Christ.

As the years went on and backers balked at escalating expenses, Gaudí sank all of his own savings into continuing the cathedral project. Work nearly ceased as Barcelona's economy collapsed and Gaudí suffered the deep personal losses of a beloved niece and his longtime companion. He grew more reclusive, and his appearance became increasingly eccentric. In fact, Gaudí may have been deep in thought about his epic construction when he walked into the path of a tram in 1926. Thousands attended his interment at La Sagrada Família.

Work resumed on the church in the 1950s and continues today, funded by private donations and admission fares. During his life, Antoni Gaudí was often ridiculed by his peers, but in death he became known as "God's Architect."

St. Peter's: Church of Churches

Sprawling across nearly six acres in the Vatican, the Basilica of Saint Peter was the world's largest Christian church for almost four centuries.

St. Peter's is not the "official" church of the pope: That honor goes to St. John Lateran. But St. Peter's is the edifice most closely identified with the papacy because its enormous size (together with St. Peter's Square out front) can accommodate tens of thousands of worshippers and pilgrims. (The term *basilica* comes from a Latinized Greek word that

describes a church built to a pattern dating back to the late Roman Empire, or a church accorded special ceremonial privileges by the pope.) The structure is built on the site on which, according to tradition, the first bishop of Rome—St. Peter, the apostle whom Jesus chose to lead the Church after his death—was crucified in the 1st century A.D.

STOREHOUSE OF MASTERPIECES

Pope Julius II laid the cornerstone for the basilica in 1506, but the structure wasn't completed until 1615, during the reign of Pope Paul V. Donato Bramante provided the original design, but after his death in 1514, a succession of architects and artists—including such great figures as Raphael and Michelangelo—worked on the project. St. Peter's eventually included Michelangelo's great sculpture the *Pietà*, as well as other important Baroque artworks, including the baldacchino (altar canopy) by Lorenzo Bernini. Within St. Peter's is the Vatican Grotto, the burial place of 91 popes (most recently Pope John Paul II in 2005) and other notables.

7 Notorious Art Thefts

Some people just can't keep their hands off other people's things—even the world's greatest art. Here are some daring thefts of very expensive art (values estimated at the time of the theft).

1. Boston, March 1990; $300 million: Two men dressed as police officers entered the Isabella Stewart Gardner Museum in the wee hours of the morning. After overpowering two guards and grabbing the surveillance tape, they collected Rembrandt's only seascape, *Storm on the Sea of Galilee*, as well as several other works. Authorities have yet to find the criminals despite investigating everyone from the Irish Republican Army to a Boston mob boss. The museum displays empty frames where the artworks once hung.

2. Oslo, August 2004; $120 million: Two armed and masked thieves threatened workers at the Munch Museum during a daring daylight theft. They stole *The Scream* and *Madonna*. In May 2006, authorities convicted three men, who each received between four and eight years in jail. The paintings were recovered three months later.

3. Paris, August 1911; $100 million: In the world's most notorious art theft to date, Vincenzo Peruggia—a Louvre employee—stole Leonardo da Vinci's *Mona Lisa*. Peruggia simply hid in a closet, grabbed the painting once alone in the room, hid it under his long smock, and walked out of the museum after it had closed. Police found Peruggia (and the *Mona Lisa*) two years later when the thief tried to sell the work to an art dealer in Florence.

4. Oslo, February 1994; $60–75 million: *The Scream* has been a popular target for thieves. Another version of Munch's famous work (he painted four) was taken from Oslo's National Art Museum. In less than one minute, the crooks came in through a window, cut the wires holding up the painting, and left through the same window. They left a piece of the frame at a bus stop, and this clue helped authorities recover the painting. Four men were convicted of the crime in January 1996.

5. Scotland, August 2003; $65 million: Two men joined a tour of Scotland's Drumlanrig Castle, subdued a guard, and made off with Leonardo da Vinci's *Madonna with the Yarnwinder*. Alarms around the art were not set during the day, and the thieves dissuaded tourists from intervening, reportedly telling them, "Don't worry . . . we're the police. This is just practice." The painting was recovered in a Glasgow law firm four years later, but the two thieves who escaped in a white Volkswagen Golf have yet to be identified.

6. Stockholm, December 2000; $30 million: Eight criminals each got up to six and half years behind bars for conspiring to take a Rembrandt and two Renoirs—all of which were eventually recovered—from Stockholm's National Museum. You have to give the three masked men who actually grabbed the paintings credit for a dramatic exit: They fled the scene by motorboat. Police unraveled the plot after recovering one of the paintings during an unrelated drug investigation.

7. Amsterdam, December 2002; $30 million: Robbers used a ladder to get onto the roof of the Van Gogh Museum, then broke in and stole two of the Dutch master's paintings—*View of the Sea at Scheveningen* and *Congregation Leaving the Reformed Church in Nuenen*. Police told the press that the thieves worked so quickly that despite setting off the museum's alarms, they had disappeared before police could get there. Two men were later caught and convicted of the theft, thanks in part to DNA left at the scene. Both paintings were discovered in 2016 by Italian police investigating suspected Italian mobsters for cocaine trafficking.

The Vanishing Treasure Room

In the Age of Enlightenment, kings and emperors built immense palaces to outdo one another—each one bigger and more gilded and bejeweled than the last. But one of Russia's greatest 18th century treasures became one of the 20th century's greatest unsolved mysteries.

The storied history of the Amber Room begins in 1701,

when it was commissioned by Frederick I of Prussia. Considered by admirers and artists alike to be the "Eighth Wonder of the World," the sparkling, honey-gold room consisted of wall panels inlaid with prehistoric amber, finely carved and illuminated by candles and mirrors. In 1716, Prussian King Freidrich Wilhelm I gifted the panels to then-ally Russian Tsar Peter the Great to ornament the imperial palace at his new capital, St. Petersburg.

After sitting at the Winter Palace for four decades, the Amber Room was moved to Tsarskoye Selo, the Romanov palace just south of St. Petersburg. During the mid-18th century, Prussia's King Frederick the Great sent Russia's Empress Elizabeth more of the amber material from his Baltic holdings, and Elizabeth ordered her court's great Italian architect, Bartolomeo Rastrelli, to expand the Amber Room into an 11-foot-square masterpiece.

The golden room was not finished until 1770, under the reign of Catherine the Great. Incorporating more than six tons of amber and accented with semiprecious stones, the fabled room became not only a prized jewel of the Russian empire, but a symbol of the long-standing alliance between Prussia and Russia.

Two centuries after the Amber Room was removed to the Tsarskoye Selo, the world was a much darker place. Prussia and Russia, formerly faithful allies, were locked in a deadly struggle that would bring down both imperial houses. By 1941, the former dominions of Frederick and Peter were ruled by Adolf Hitler and Joseph Stalin.

In a surprise attack, Hitler's armies drove across the Soviet border in June 1941. German panzers drove from the Polish frontier to the gates of Moscow in an epic six-month campaign, devouring some of the most fertile, productive territory in Eastern Europe.

AN ATTEMPT TO COVER

One of the unfortunate cities in the path of the Nazi onslaught was St. Petersburg, renamed Leningrad by its communist masters. Frantic palace curators desperately tried to remove the Amber Room's antique panels, but the brittle prehistoric resin began to crumble as the panels were detached. Faced with probable destruction of one of Russia's greatest treasures or its abandonment to the Nazis, the curators attempted to hide the room's precious panels by covering them with gauze and wallpaper.

Although Leningrad withstood a long, bloody siege, German troops swept through the city's suburbs, capturing Tsarskoye Selo intact in October 1941. Soldiers discovered the treasure hidden behind the wallpaper, and German troops disassembled the room's panels over a 36-hour period, packed them in 27 crates, and shipped them back to Königsberg, in East Prussia.

The fabled Amber Room panels were put on display in Königsberg's castle museum. They remained there for two years—until the Third Reich began to crumble before the weight of Soviet and Anglo-American military forces. Sometime in 1944, the room's valuable panels were allegedly dismantled and packed into crates, to prevent damage by British and Soviet bombers. In January 1945, Hitler permitted the westward movement of cultural treasures, including the Italo-Russo-German masterpiece.

And from there, the Amber Room was lost to history.

THE GREAT TREASURE HUNT

The world was left to speculate about the fate of the famous imperial room, and dozens of theories have been spawned about the room's whereabouts. Some claim the Amber Room was lost—sunk aboard a submarine, bombed to pieces, or perhaps burned in Königsberg. This last conclusion was accepted by Alexander Brusov, a Soviet investigator sent to find the Amber Room shortly after war's end. Referring to the destruction of Königsberg Castle by Red Army forces on April 9, 1945, he concluded: "Summarizing all the facts, we can say that the Amber Room was destroyed between 9 and 11 April 1945." An in-depth hunt by two British investigative journalists pieced together the last days of the Amber Room and concluded that its fate was sealed when Soviet troops accidentally set fire to the castle compound during the last month of combat, destroying the brittle jewels and obscuring their location.

Other treasure hunters, however, claim the room still sits in an abandoned mine shaft or some long-forgotten Nazi bunker beneath the outskirts of Königsberg. One German investigator claimed former SS officers told him the room's panels were packed up and hidden in an abandoned silver mine near Berlin; a Lithuanian official claimed witnesses saw SS troops hiding the panels in a local swamp. Neither has been able to prove his claims.

THE TRAIL GOES COLD

The hunt for the Amber Room has been made more difficult because its last witnesses are gone—several under mysterious circumstances. General Gusev, a Soviet intelligence officer who spoke to a journalist about the room's whereabouts, died in a car crash the day after their conversation. In 1987, Georg Stein, a former German soldier who had devoted his life to searching for the Amber Room, was found murdered in a forest, his stomach slit open by a scalpel.

In 1997, the world got a tantalizing glimpse of the long-lost treasure when German police raided the office of a Bremen lawyer who was attempting to sell an amber mosaic worth $2.5 million on behalf of one of his clients, the son of a former German lieutenant. The small mosaic—inlaid with jade and onyx as well as amber—had been stolen from the Amber Room by a German officer and was separated from the main panels. After its seizure, this last true remnant of the legendary tsarist treasure made its way back to Russia in April 2000.

Decades of searches by German and Soviet investigators have come up empty. The fate of the fabled room—worth an estimated $142 million to $250 million in today's currency—has remained an elusive ghost for treasure seekers, mystery writers, and investigators looking for the Holy Grail of Russian baroque artwork.

In 1979, the Soviet government, with help from a donation made by a German gas firm in 1999, began amassing old photographs of the Amber Room and pieces of the rare amber to create a reconstructed room worthy of its predecessor. Carefully rebuilt at a cost exceeding $7 million, the reconstructed room was dedicated by the Russian president and German chancellor at a ceremony in 2003, marking the tricentennial of St. Petersburg's founding. The dazzling Amber Room is now on display for tourists who come to Tsarskoye Selo to view the playground of one of Europe's great dynasties.

The Profound Effect of *Uncle Tom's Cabin*

When Harriet Beecher Stowe was introduced to President Abraham Lincoln, as the story goes, he said, "So, you're the little woman who wrote the book that started this great war." There's no question that few elements fueled the flames of hate across the country as much as *Uncle Tom's Cabin*. Stowe's story of Tom, a saintly black slave, earned both praise and condemnation. Abolitionists across the North thought it was brilliant and oh, so true. Southern critics, however, complained that it was completely inaccurate in the way it portrayed plantation life.

BORROWING FROM REAL LIFE

Stowe was a dedicated abolitionist who was more concerned about illustrating the evils of slavery than creating an accurate view of life on the plantation. Although she lived in Cincinnati, Ohio (just across the river from the slave state of Kentucky), she had little actual experience with Southern plantations. The information in most of her book was taken either from abolitionist literature or her own imagination.

Stowe was researching a series of articles she intended to write when she heard about a slave woman who escaped from her masters in Kentucky across a frozen Ohio River. Stowe immediately realized that she could use such a scene in a book. One of the most exciting parts of *Uncle Tom's Cabin* features Eliza, the slave heroine, escaping across the ice.

A PUBLISHING SENSATION

Uncle Tom's Cabin first appeared in 1851, serialized in the abolitionist newspaper *National Era*. Its popularity led to the book's publication as a complete work the next year. It was an instant success, selling 10,000 copies in the first week and more than 300,000 by the end of its first year. *Uncle Tom's Cabin* had even greater popularity in Britain, where more than one million copies sold within a year. Stowe exposed the general public to an issue that most knew very little about. But the book didn't simply educate its readers—it also provoked heated debates in state and federal legislatures.

Interestingly, given today's negative meaning of the term Uncle Tom, the character in Stowe's book demonstrated strength and traits that were quite heroic. In one instance, when ordered to whip a sickly female slave, Tom refuses and suffers the lash himself. He is ultimately killed by his wicked master, Simon Legree, because he will not betray two runaway slaves. When Legree tries to have the information beaten out of him, Tom goes to his death without revealing a thing.

NOT CONTROVERSIAL ENOUGH?

As shocking as a lot of people found *Uncle Tom's Cabin*, many—particularly radical abolitionists—didn't think the book went far enough in denouncing slavery. Others, usually those who lived in the South, condemned the book as grossly exaggerated. One of Stowe's admirers was William Lloyd Garrison, the editor of an abolitionist newspaper called *The Liberator*. "I estimate the value of antislavery writing by the abuse it brings," he wrote to tell her. "Now all the defenders of slavery have let me alone and are abusing you."

Going Under the Knife to Hit the High Notes

"Mutilated for their art" is how one period writer praised the castrati, male sopranos and alto-sopranos whose manhood was intentionally removed before puberty to keep their voices "sweet."

Putting young boys under the knife to create a corps of eunuchs had been done since antiquity. While the practice was applied by the Byzantine, Ottoman, and Chinese to create castes of priests, civil servants, and harem guards, the Italians of the 16th century used it to populate their church choirs.

Young boys can hit high notes for only so long before hormones kick in and thicken the vocal cords. Late Renaissance Italians, with the blessing of a Papal Bull from 1589, preempted this progression of nature. Priests and choirmasters recruited boys, and parents sold or volunteered their sons (often as young as eight years old) to undergo castration. The removal of their testicles ensured that the boys would keep their sweet, angelic voices—voices that, as they grew into men, would become stronger and louder and more powerful without dropping in tone and timbre. Castrati had the "chest of man and the voice of a woman," as one enthusiastic supporter of the practice observed.

The Italians were not the first to introduce prepubescent emasculation in the name of art. Byzantine Empress Eudoxia first sanctioned this practice in A.D. 400 at the urging of her choirmaster, Brison, but the practice soon fell out of favor. Even so, as the Renaissance and the golden age of church music dawned, the castration of young boys began to occur with regularity throughout Europe, particularly in Germany. It was in Italy, however, where it became something of a mania and where it continued for the longest amount of time.

By the late 18th century, as many as 4,000 boys a year were inducted into the ranks of the castrati in Italy alone—an especially staggering statistic considering the crude medical practices and almost complete lack of anesthesia of the era. (Some patients were given drink and opium before the procedure, however.)

TAKING TO THE STAGE

Castrati also appeared in plays, taking female roles at a time when women were still banned from performing in public. Although most castrati never left the choir, the popularization and proliferation of opera in the 17th, 18th, and 19th centuries gave them a new stage on which to showcase their talents. Opera castrati were the superstars of their era; noted composers wrote lead roles for them. Prized for the power and pitch of their angelic voices, the best of them were the toast of Europe, courted by kings, praised by artists, and sought after by women.

The revolutions that rocked Europe eventually turned public opinion against the practice. At first only frowned upon, it was soon banned by law. Italy, in 1870, was the last of the European countries to enact such legislation. The Catholic Church, however, continued to welcome castrati into church choirs until 1902, and it was not until the following year that Pope Leo XIII revoked the Papal Bull of 1589.

Even as their ranks thinned, cries of *eviva il coltello* or "long live the knife" continued to resound for these aging stars when they performed. Castrati hit the high notes right up until the eve of the First World War. Alessandro Moreschi, who retired in 1913, was the last of the castrati. His angelic falsetto has been preserved in a rare recording made in 1902.

CHAPTER 10

CRIME

The Lizzie Borden Murder Mystery

Most people know the rhyme that begins, "Lizzie Borden took an ax and gave her mother 40 whacks . . ." In reality, approximately 20 hatchet chops cut down Abby Borden, but no matter the number, Lizzie's stepmother was very much dead on that sultry August morning in 1892. Lizzie's father, Andrew, was killed about an hour later. His life was cut short by about a dozen hatchet chops to the head. No one knows who was guilty of these murders, but Lizzie has always carried the burden of suspicion.

ANDREW BORDEN, AN AMERICAN "SCROOGE"

Andrew Jackson Borden was one of the richest men in Fall River, Massachusetts, with a net worth of nearly half a million dollars. In 1892, that was enormous wealth. Andrew was a shrewd businessman: At the time of his death, he was the president of the Union Savings Bank and director of another bank and several profitable cotton mills.

Despite his wealth, Andrew was miserly. Though some of his neighbors' homes had running hot water, the three-story Borden home had just two cold-water taps, and there was no water available above the first floor. The Bordens' only latrine was in the cellar, so they generally used chamber pots that were either dumped onto the lawn behind the house or emptied into the cellar toilet. And, although most wealthy people used gas lighting, the Bordens lit their house with inexpensive kerosene lamps.

Worst of all, for many years, Andrew was an undertaker who offered some of the lowest prices in town. He worked on the bodies in the basement of the Borden home, and allegedly, he bent the knees of the deceased (and in some cases, cut off their feet) to fit the bodies into smaller, less expensive coffins in order to increase his business.

So despite the brutality of Andrew's murder, it seems few people mourned his loss. The question wasn't why he was killed, but who did it.

LIZZIE VS. WILLIAM

In 1997, when psychic Jane Doherty visited the murder site, she uncovered several clues about the Lizzie Borden case. Doherty felt that the real murderer was someone named "Willie." There is no real evidence to support this claim, but some believe Andrew had an illegitimate son named William who spent time as an inmate in an insane asylum. His constant companion was reportedly his hatchet, which he talked to as though it were a friend. Also, at least one witness reportedly saw William at the Borden house on the day of the murders. William was supposedly there to challenge Andrew about his new will.

Was William the killer? A few years after the murders, William took poison and then hung himself in the woods. Near his swinging body, he'd reportedly left his hatchet on the ground. So with William dead and Lizzie already acquitted, the Borden murder case was put to rest.

LIZZIE'S FORBIDDEN ROMANCE

One of the most curious explanations for the murder involves the Bordens' servant Bridget Sullivan. Her participation has always raised questions. Like the other members of the Borden household, Bridget had suffered from apparent food poisoning the night before the murders. She claimed to have been ill in the backyard of the Borden home.

During the time Lizzie's stepmother Abby was being murdered, Bridget was apparently washing windows in the back of the house. Later, when Andrew was killed, Bridget was resting in her room upstairs. Why didn't she hear two people being butchered?

According to some theories, Lizzie and Bridget had been romantically involved. In this version of the story, their relationship was discovered shortly before the murders. Around this same time, Andrew was reportedly rewriting his will. His wife was now "Mrs. Borden," to Lizzie, not "Mother," as Lizzie had called her stepmother for many years. The reason for the estrangement was never clear.

Lizzie also had a strange relationship with her father and had given him her high school ring, as though he were her sweetheart. He wore the ring on his pinky finger and was buried with it.

Just a day before the murders, Lizzie had been attempting to purchase prussic acid—a deadly poison—and the family came down with "food poisoning" that night.

Some speculate that Bridget was Lizzie's accomplice in the murders and helped clean up the blood afterward.

This theory was bolstered when, a few years after the murders, Lizzie became involved with actress Nance O'Neil. For two years, Lizzie and the statuesque actress were inseparable. This prompted Emma Borden, Lizzie's sister, to move out of their home.

At the time, the rift between the sisters sparked rumors that either Lizzie or Emma might reveal more about the other's role in the 1892 murders. However, neither of them said anything new about the killings.

WHODUNIT?

Most people believe that Lizzie was the killer. She was the only one accused of the crime, for several good reasons: Lizzie appeared to be the only one in the house at the time. She showed no signs of grief when the murders were discovered. During questioning, Lizzie changed her story several times. The evidence was entirely circumstantial, but it was compelling enough to go to trial.

Ultimately, the jury accepted her attorney's closing argument, that the murders were "morally and physically impossible for this young woman defendant." In other words, Lizzie had to be innocent because she was petite and well bred. In 19th-century New England, that seemed like a logical and persuasive defense. Lizzie went free, and no one else was charged with the crimes.

But Lizzie wasn't the only one with motive, means, and opportunity. The most likely suspects were family members, working alone or with other relatives. Only a few had solid alibis, and—like Lizzie—many changed their stories during police questioning. But there was never enough evidence to officially accuse anyone other than Lizzie.

So whether or not Lizzie Borden "took an ax" and killed her parents, she's the one most closely associated with the crime.

LIZZIE BORDEN BED & BREAKFAST

The Borden house has been sold several times over the years, but today it is a bed-and-breakfast—the main draw, of course, being the building's macabre history. The Victorian residence has been restored to reflect the details of the Borden home at the time of the murders, including the couch on which Andrew lay, his skull hideously smashed.

As a guest, you can stay in one of six rooms, even the one in which Abby was murdered. Then, after a good night's sleep, you'll be treated to a breakfast reminiscent of the one the Bordens had on their final morning in 1892. That is, if you got to sleep at all. (They say the place is haunted.)

As with all good morbid attractions, the proprietors at the Lizzie Borden B&B don't take themselves too seriously. Before you leave, you can stop by the gift shop and pick up a pair of hatchet earrings, an "I Survived the Night at the Lizzie Borden Bed & Breakfast" T-shirt, or an ax-wielding Lizzie Borden bobble-head doll.

Ponzi: The Man and the Scam

Do you want to get rich quick? Are you charming and persuasive? Do you lack scruples? Do you have a relaxed attitude toward the law? If so, the Ponzi Scheme may be for you!

Yes, there was a real Mr. Ponzi, and here's how his scam worked. First, come up with a phony investment—it could be a parcel of (worthless) land that you're sure is going to rise in value in a few months or stock in a (nonexistent) company that you're certain is going to go through the roof soon. Then recruit a small group of investors, promising to, say, double their money in 90 days. Ninety days later, send these initial investors (or at least some of them) a check for double their investment. They'll be so pleased, they'll tell everyone they know about this surefire way to make a fast buck.

You use the influx of cash from the new investors to pay your initial investors—those who ask for a payout, that is. The beauty of it is that most of your initial investors will be so enchanted with those first checks that they'll beg to reinvest their money with you. Eventually, of course, your new investors will start to wonder why they aren't getting any checks, and/or some government agency or reporter might come snooping around . . . but by then (if you've timed it right) you'll have transferred yourself and your ill-gotten gains out of the reach of the authorities. Like related scams that include the Pyramid Scheme and the Stock Bubble, financial frauds like this one have been around for centuries, but only the Ponzi Scheme bears the name of a particular individual—Charles Ponzi.

As you might imagine—given that he was a legendary con man—Ponzi gave differing accounts of his background, so it's hard to establish facts about his early life. He was likely born Carlos Ponzi in Italy in 1882. He came to America in 1903 and lived the hardscrabble existence of a newly arrived immigrant. But the handsome, suave Ponzi was determined to rise in the world—by fair means or foul. The foul means included bank fraud and immigrant smuggling, and Ponzi wound up doing time in jails in both the United States and Canada.

THE CHECK IS (NOT) IN THE MAIL

While living in Boston in 1919, the newly freed Ponzi more or less stumbled across the scheme that would earn him notoriety. It involved an easily obtained item called an International Postal Reply Coupon. In simple terms, the scam involved using foreign currencies to purchase quantities of a kind of international postal stamp, then redeeming the stamps for U.S. dollars. This brought a big profit because of the favorable exchange rate of the time, and it actually wasn't illegal. The illegal part was Ponzi's determination to bring ever-growing numbers of investors into the scheme . . . and just keep their money. Until the roof fell in, Ponzi became a celebrity. Before long, people across New England and beyond were withdrawing their life savings and mortgaging their homes to get in on the action.

The end came in the summer of 1920, when a series of investigative reports in a Boston newspaper revealed that the House of Ponzi had no foundations. By that time, he'd taken some 40,000 people for a total of about $15 million. In 21st-century terms, that's roughly $150 million. Ponzi spent a dozen years in prison on mail fraud charges. Upon release, he was deported and continued his scamming ways abroad before dying penniless in Brazil in 1948.

The Bloody Countess

In the early 1600s, villagers in the Carpathian region of Hungary whispered amongst themselves about a vampire living in the local castle. An investigation brought to light the brutal atrocities of Countess Elizabeth Báthory, who was accused of torturing hundreds of young girls to death and bathing in their blood.

THE BEST SORT OF PEOPLE

Elizabeth Báthory (born Erzsébet Báthory in 1560) was the daughter of one of the oldest and most influential bloodlines in Hungary. Her wedding in 1575 to Ferenc Nádasdy was enough of an event to warrant written approval and an expensive gift from the Holy Roman Emperor himself.

There were rumors that a streak of insanity ran in Elizabeth's family; some rumors hinted that she may have been related to Vlad the Impaler. However, nobles of the time were given wide latitude when it came to eccentric behavior.

Ferenc would go on to become one of the greatest Hungarian military heroes of the age. He was a battle-hardened man, but his wife treated the servants even more harshly than he did—and he had no reservations when it came to punishing the help. He was known to place flaming oil-covered wicks between the toes of lazy servants. But Elizabeth's punishments exceeded even this brutality. One honey-covered servant had been tied to a tree and ravaged by ants as punishment for stealing food. Ferenc spent a great deal of time away at war, and someone had to manage his castle. Elizabeth took on the task willingly.

Initially, Elizabeth's punishments may have been no harsher than those imposed by her contemporaries. However, with her husband's lengthy absences and eventual death, Elizabeth found that she had virtually no restrictions on her behavior. She dabbled in black magic and had a series of lovers (legend has it one was the devil himself!).

Elizabeth spent hours doing nothing more than gazing into a wraparound mirror of her own design, crafted to hold her upright so that she would not tire as she examined her own reflection. Always a vain woman, the exacting fashion of the day required Elizabeth to constantly worry over the angle of her collar or the style of her hair. She had a small army of servants constantly by her side to help maintain her appearance. If they failed in their duties, Elizabeth would strike out and pummel them to the ground. On one occasion, a servant pulled too hard when combing Elizabeth's hair; Elizabeth struck the offender in the face hard enough to cause the girl's blood to spray and cover the countess. Initially furious, Elizabeth discovered she liked the sensation and began to use it as part of her spells.

CRIMES MOST FOUL

The incident led to egregious atrocities. One story has her inviting 60 peasant girls (selected for their youth, beauty, and soft skin) for a banquet, only to lock them in a room and slaughter them one at a time. The countess began torturing girls without restraint. Aided by two trustworthy servants who recruited a never-ending supply of hopeful girls from the poor families of the area, she would beat her victims with a club until they were scarcely recognizable. When her arms grew tired, she had her two assistants continue the punishment as she watched. She had a spiked iron cage specially built and would place a girl within it, shaking the cage as the individual bounced from side to side and was repeatedly impaled on the spikes. She drove pins into lips and breasts, sewed mouths shut, held flames to pubic regions, and once pulled a victim's mouth open so forcefully that the girl's cheeks split.

Perhaps most chillingly, allegations of vampirism and cannibalism arose when Elizabeth began biting her victims, tearing off the flesh with her bare teeth. On one occasion, too sick to rise from her bed, the countess demanded that a peasant girl be brought to her. She roused herself long enough to bite chunks from the girl's face, shoulders, and nipples. She forced one young woman to strip her own flesh. Elizabeth's chambers had to be covered with fresh cinders daily to prevent the countess from slipping on the bloody floor.

THE COUNTESS ON TRIAL

Eventually, even the cloak of nobility couldn't hide Elizabeth's atrocities. The situation was compounded by the fact that she got sloppy, killing in such numbers that the local clergy refused to perform any more burials. Thereafter, she would throw bodies to the wolves in full view of local villagers, who naturally complained to the authorities. The final straw was when Elizabeth began to prey on the minor aristocracy as well as the peasants; the disappearance of people of higher birth could not be tolerated.

The king decided that something had to be done, and in January 1611, a trial was held. Elizabeth was not allowed to testify, but her assistants were compelled to—condemning themselves to death in the process—and they provided eyewitness accounts of the terrible practices of the countess. Especially damning was the discovery of a list, in Elizabeth's own handwriting, describing more than 600 people she had tortured to death.

Elizabeth Bathory was convicted of perpetrating "horrifying cruelties" and was sentenced to be walled up alive in her own castle. She survived for nearly four years but was finally discovered dead on August 21, 1614, by one of her guards who had risked a peek through a tiny food slot. The countess was unrepentant to the end.

Real Manchurian Candidates

From the mid-1950s through at least the early 1970s, thousands of unwitting Americans and Canadians became part of a bizarre CIA research project codenamed MKULTRA. Participants were secretly "brainwashed"—drugged with LSD and other hallucinogens, subjected to electroconvulsive shock therapy, and manipulated with abusive mind-control techniques.

MKULTRA began in 1953 under the orders of CIA director Allen Dulles. The program was developed in response to reports that U.S. prisoners of war in Korea were being subjected to mind-control techniques.

CIA researchers hoped to find a "truth drug" that could be used on Soviet agents, as well as drugs that could be used against foreign leaders (one documented scheme involved an attempt in 1960 to dose Fidel Castro with LSD). They also aimed to develop means of mind control that would benefit U.S. intelligence, perhaps including the creation of so-called "Manchurian Candidates" to carry out assassinations. The CIA investigated parapsychology and such phenomena as hypnosis, telepathy, precognition, photokinesis, and "remote viewing."

MKULTRA was headed by Sidney Gottlieb, a military psychiatrist and chemist who specialized in concocting deadly poisons. More than 30 universities and scientific institutes took part in MKULTRA. LSD and other mind-altering drugs including heroin, mescaline, psilocybin, scopolamine, marijuana, and sodium pentothal were given to CIA employees, military personnel, and other government workers, often without the subjects' knowledge or consent.

To broaden their subject pool, researchers targeted unsuspecting civilians, often those in vulnerable or socially compromising situations. Inmates, prostitutes, and the mentally ill were often used. In a project codenamed Operation Midnight Climax, the CIA set up brothels in several U.S. cities to lure men as unwitting test subjects. Rooms were equipped with cameras that filmed the experiments behind one-way mirrors. Some civilian subjects who consented to participation were used for more extreme experimentation. One group of volunteers in Kentucky was given LSD for more than 70 straight days.

CLANDESTINE RESEARCH

Gottlieb conducted mind-control experiments on POWs held by U.S. forces in Vietnam. During the same time period, an unknown number of Soviet agents died in U.S. custody in Europe after being given dual intravenous injections of barbiturates and amphetamine in the CIA's search for a truth serum.

MKULTRA experiments were also carried out in Montreal, Canada, between 1957 and 1964 by Donald Ewen Cameron, a researcher in Albany, New York, who also served as president of the World Psychiatric Association. The CIA appears to have given him potentially deadly experiments to carry out in Canada so U.S. citizens would not be involved.

Cameron also experimented with paralytic drugs as well as using electroconvulsive therapy at 30 times the normal voltage. The subjects were often women being treated for anxiety disorders. Many suffered permanent damage. A lawsuit by victims of the experiments later uncovered that the Canadian government had also funded the project.

There was at least one American casualty of the experiments. Frank Olson, a biological weapons researcher, was found dead on a New York City sidewalk in 1953. A doctor assigned to monitor Olson claimed he jumped from the window of his 10th-floor hotel room. Understandably, Olson's family had trouble making sense of the events. Declassified documents later revealed that Olson had been secretly dosed with LSD prior to his untimely death. Olson's family had his body exhumed in 1994.

An autopsy revealed that Olson had been knocked unconscious before his fall, leading his family to believe that someone threw Olson out the window. His family believes Olson was considered a security risk because he had witnessed some unethical experiments and was no longer proud of his work.

The U.S. army also conducted experiments with psychoactive drugs. A later investigation determined most army experiments involved subjects who had given their consent, and army researchers largely followed safety protocols. Ken Kesey, who later wrote *One Flew Over the Cuckoo's Nest*, volunteered for LSD studies at an army research center in San Francisco in 1960.

The army's high ethical standards seem to have been absent in at least one case. Harold Blauer, a professional tennis player in New York City who was hospitalized for depression following his divorce, died from apparent cardiac arrest during an army experiment in 1952. Blauer had been secretly injected with massive doses of mescaline.

CIA researchers eventually concluded that the effects of LSD were too unpredictable to be useful, and the agency later acknowledged that their experiments made little scientific sense. Records on 150 MKULTRA research projects were destroyed in 1973 by order of CIA Director Richard Helms. A year later, *The New York Times* first reported about CIA experiments on U.S. citizens. In 1975, congressional hearings and a report by the Rockefeller Commission revealed details of the program. In 1976, President Gerald Ford issued an executive order prohibiting experimentation with drugs on human subjects without their informed consent. Ford and CIA Director William Colby also publicly apologized to Frank Olson's family, who received $750,000 by a special act of Congress.

Murder in the Heartland

If you ever find yourself in northwestern Kansas looking for the village of Holcomb, don't blink or you'll miss it. It's the kind of place where nothing ever seems to happen. And yet, back in 1959, Holcomb became one of the most notorious locations in the history of American crime.

In the 1940s, businessman Herb Clutter built a house on the outskirts of Holcomb and started raising a family with his wife, Bonnie. The Clutters were friendly and quickly became one of the most popular families in the small village.

On the morning of Sunday, November 15, 1959, Clarence Ewalt drove his daughter Nancy to the Clutter house so she could go to church with the family as she did every week. She was a good friend of the Clutters' teenage daughter, who was also named Nancy. Nancy Ewalt knocked on the door several times but got no response. She went around to a side door, looked around and called out, but no one answered.

Mr. Ewalt drove his daughter to the Kidwell house nearby and picked up Susan Kidwell, another friend. Susan tried phoning the Clutters, but no one answered. So the three drove back to the Clutter house. The two girls entered the house through the kitchen door and went to Nancy Clutter's room, where they found the dead body of their dear friend.

UNSPEAKABLE ACTS

Sheriff Robinson—the first officer to respond—entered the house with another officer and Larry Hendricks, a neighbor of the Clutters. The three men went first to Nancy Clutter's room, where the teenager was dead of a gunshot wound to the head. She was lying on her bed facing the wall with her hands and ankles bound. Bonnie Clutter was discovered in the master bedroom. Like her daughter, Bonnie's hands and feet were bound, and she appeared to have been shot in the head.

Police found the bodies of Herb Clutter and his 15-year-old son, Kenyon, in the basement. Like his mother and sister, Kenyon had been shot in the head; his body was tied to a sofa.

Herb Clutter appeared to have suffered the most. He had also been shot in the head, but there were slash marks on his throat, and his mouth was taped shut. And although his body was lying on the floor of the basement, there was a rope hanging from the ceiling; between that and the marks on Herb's neck, investigators surmised Herb had been hung from the rope at some point.

DEWEY'S TASK FORCE

Alvin A. Dewey of the Kansas City Bureau of Investigation (KBI) took charge of the investigation. The Clutter murders hit Dewey hard. The Dewey and Clutter families had attended the same church, and Dewey considered Herb a good friend.

At the press conference after the bodies were discovered, Dewey announced that his task force would not rest until they found the person or persons responsible for the horrific murders. He knew it was going to be a tough case, though. The gore at the scene suggested a motive of revenge. But the Clutters were loved by all, as evidenced by the nearly 600 mourners who showed up for the funeral service. The idea that the murders were the result of a robbery gone bad was also being pursued, but Dewey had his doubts about that. It just didn't fit that the entire Clutter family would have walked in on a robbery and then been killed the way they had. Dewey began to believe that there had been more than one killer.

There was not a lot of evidence. Not only was the weapon missing, the perpetrator had taken the time to pick up the spent shells. However, Dewey did have a secret ace up his sleeve: Herb Clutter's body had been found lying on a piece of cardboard, and on that cardboard were impressions from a man's boot. Both Herb and Kenyon were barefoot, which meant the boots may have belonged to the killer. It wasn't much, but it was a start. Still, as Christmas crept closer, the case was starting to come to a standstill. Then, finally, a big break came from an unlikely place: Lansing Prison.

AN INMATE TALKS

The man who would break the case wide open was Lansing Prison inmate Floyd Wells. Earlier in the year, Wells had been sentenced to Lansing for breaking and entering. His cellmate was a man named Richard Hickock. One night, Hickock mentioned that even though he was going to be released from prison soon, he had nowhere to go. Wells told him that back in the late 1940s, he had been out looking for work and stumbled across a kind, rich man named Clutter who would often hire people to work around his farm. Once Wells mentioned Herb Clutter, Hickock seemed obsessed with the man. He wouldn't stop asking questions: How old was he? Was he strong? How many others lived in the house?

One night, Hickock calmly stated that when he was released, he and his friend Perry Smith were going to rob the Clutters and murder anyone in the house. Wells said that Hickock even explained exactly how he would tie everyone up and shoot them one at a time. Wells further stated that he never believed Hickock was serious until he heard that the Clutters had been murdered in exactly the way Hickock had described.

On December 30, after attempting to cash a series of bad checks, Hickock and Smith were arrested in Las Vegas. Among the items seized from the stolen car they were driving was a pair of boots belonging to Hickock. When confronted with the fact that his boots matched the imprint at the crime scene, Hickock broke down and admitted he had been there during the murders. However, he swore that Perry Smith had killed the whole family and that he had tried to stop him.

When Smith was informed that his partner was putting all the blame on him, Smith gave a very detailed version of how Hickock had devised a plan to steal the contents of a safe in Herb Clutter's home office. The pair had crept in through an unlocked door at approximately 12:30 A.M. Finding no safe, the pair went to the master bedroom, where they surprised a sleeping Herb Clutter. When told they had come for the contents of the safe, Herb told them to take whatever they wanted, but there was no safe in the house. Not convinced, Smith and Hickock rounded up the family and tied them up, hoping to get one of them to reveal the location of the safe. When that failed, Smith and Hickock prepared to leave. But when Hickock started bragging about how he had been ready to kill the entire family, Smith called his bluff, and an argument ensued. At that point, Smith said he snapped and stabbed Herb Clutter in the throat. Seeing the man in such pain, Smith said he then shot him to end his suffering. Smith then turned the gun on Kenyon. Smith ended his statement by saying that he'd made Hickock kill the two women.

THE VERDICT

The trial of Richard Hickock and Perry Smith began on March 23, 1960, at Finney County Courthouse. Five days later, the case was handed over to the jury, who needed only 40 minutes to reach their verdict: Both men were guilty of all charges. They recommended that Hickock and Smith be hanged for their crimes.

Sitting in the front row when the verdicts were read was Truman Capote, who had been writing a series of articles about the murders for *The New Yorker*. Those articles would later inspire his best-selling novel *In Cold Blood*.

After several appeals, both men were executed at Lansing Prison on April 14, 1965. Richard Hickock was the first to be hanged, with Perry Smith going to the same gallows roughly 30 minutes later. Agent Alvin Dewey was present for both executions.

Several years after the murders, in an attempt to heal the community, a stained-glass window at the First Methodist Church in Garden City, Kansas, was dedicated to the Clutters. Despite an initial impulse to bulldoze the Clutter house, it was left standing and is a private residence today.

9 of History's Coldest Cases

They were gruesome crimes that shocked us with their brutality. But as time passed, we heard less and less about them because the killers left frustratingly few clues behind.

1. Jack the Ripper: A brutal killer known as Jack the Ripper preyed on London prostitutes in the late 1880s. His first victim was 43-year-old Mary Ann Nichols, who was nearly decapitated. Days later, 47-year-old Annie Chapman had her organs removed before being left for dead. Three weeks later, the killer was interrupted as he tore apart Swedish prostitute Elizabeth Stride. He managed to get away, only to strike again that same night. This time the victim was Kate Eddowes. His final kill was the most gruesome. On the night of November 9, 1888, Mary Kelly was methodically cut into pieces in an onslaught that must have lasted for several hours.

Dozens of potential Jacks (and even one Jill) have been implicated in the killings, including midwife Mary Pearcey and morgue attendant Robert Mann. But more than

130 years after the savage attacks, the identity of Jack the Ripper remains a mystery.

2. The Torso Killer: In Cleveland, Ohio, during the 1930s, more than a dozen limbless torsos were found. Despite the efforts of famed crime fighter Eliot Ness, the torso killer was never found. The first two bodies, found in September 1935, were missing heads and had been horribly mutilated. Similar murders occurred during the next three years. Desperate to stop the killings, Ness ordered a raid on a run-down area known as Kingsbury's Run, where most of the victims were from. The place was torched, and hundreds of vagrants were taken into custody. After that, there were no more killings.

The key suspect in the murders was Frank Dolezal, a vagrant who lived in the area. He was a known bully with a fiery temper. Dolezal was arrested and subsequently confessed, but his confession was full of inaccuracies. He died shortly thereafter under suspicious circumstances.

3. Elizabeth Short: Elizabeth Short, also known as the Black Dahlia, was murdered in 1947. Like thousands of others, Elizabeth wanted to be a star. Unlike the bevy of blondes who trekked to Hollywood, this 22-year-old beauty from Massachusetts was dark and mysterious. She was last seen alive outside the Biltmore Hotel in Los Angeles on the evening of January 9, 1947.

Short's body was found on a vacant lot in Los Angeles. It had been cut in half at the waist and both parts had been drained of blood and then cleaned. Her body parts appeared to be surgically dissected, and her remains were suggestively posed. Despite receiving a number of false confessions and taunting letters that admonished police to "catch me if you can," the crime remains unsolved.

4. The Zodiac Killer: The Zodiac Killer was responsible for several murders in the San Francisco area in the 1960s and 1970s. His victims were shot, stabbed, and bludgeoned to death. After the first few kills, he began sending letters to the local press in which he taunted police and made threats, such as planning to blow up a school bus. In a letter sent to the *San Francisco Chronicle* two days after the murder of cabbie Paul Stine in October 1969, the killer, who called himself "The Zodiac," included in the package pieces of Stine's blood-soaked shirt. In the letters, which continued until 1978, he claimed a cumulative tally of 37 murders.

5. Jimmy Hoffa: In 1975, labor leader Jimmy Hoffa disappeared on his way to a Detroit-area restaurant. Hoffa was the president of the Teamsters Union during the 1950s and 1960s. In 1964, he went to jail for bribing a grand juror investigating corruption in the union. In 1971, he was released on the condition that he not participate in any further union activity. Hoffa was preparing a legal challenge to that injunction when he disappeared on July 30, 1975. He was last seen in the parking lot of the Machus Red Fox restaurant.

Hoffa had strong connections to the Mafia, and several mobsters have claimed that he met a grisly end on their say-so. Although his body has never been found, authorities officially declared him dead on July 30, 1982. In November 2006, the FBI dug up farmland in Michigan hoping to turn up a corpse. So far, no luck.

6. Bob Crane: In 1978, Bob Crane, star of TV's *Hogan's Heroes*, was clubbed to death in his apartment. Crane shared a close friendship with John Carpenter, a pioneer in the development of video technology. The two shared an affinity for debauchery and sexual excesses, which they often recorded on videotape. But by late 1978,

Crane was tiring of Carpenter's dependence on him and had ended the relationship.

On June 29, 1978, Crane was bludgeoned to death with a camera tripod in his Scottsdale, Arizona, apartment. Suspicion immediately fell on Carpenter. A small spattering of blood was found in Carpenter's rental car, but police were unable to connect it to the crime. Examiners also found a tiny piece of human tissue in the car. Sixteen years after the killing, Carpenter finally went to trial, but he was acquitted due to lack of evidence.

7. Swedish Prime Minister Olof Palme: On February 28, 1986, Swedish Prime Minister Olof Palme was gunned down on a Stockholm street as he and his wife strolled home from the movies unprotected around midnight. The prime minister was fatally shot in the back. His wife was seriously wounded but survived.

In 1988, a petty thief and drug addict named Christer Petterson was convicted of the murder because he was picked out of a lineup by Palme's widow. The conviction was later overturned on appeal when doubts were raised as to the reliability of Mrs. Palme's evidence. Despite many theories, the assassin remains at large.

8. Tupac Shakur: On September 7, 1996, rapper Tupac Shakur was shot four times in a drive-by shooting in Las Vegas. He died six days later. Two years prior to that, Shakur had been shot five times in the lobby of a Manhattan recording studio the day before he was found guilty of sexual assault. The 1994 shooting was a major catalyst for an East Coast-West Coast feud that would envelop the hip-hop industry and culminate in the deaths of both Shakur and Notorious B.I.G. (Christopher Wallace).

On the night of the fatal shooting, Shakur attended the Mike Tyson-Bruce Seldon fight at the MGM Grand in Las Vegas. After the fight, Shakur and his entourage got into a scuffle. Shakur then headed for a nightclub, but he never made it. No one was ever arrested for the killing.

9. JonBenét Ramsey: On the morning of December 26, 1996, Patsy Ramsey found a ransom note that indicated that JonBenét, her six-year-old daughter, had been abducted from her Boulder, Colorado, home. Police rushed to the Ramsey home where, hours later, John Ramsey found his little girl dead in the basement. She had been battered, sexually assaulted, and strangled.

Police found several tantalizing bits of evidence—a number of footprints, a rope that did not belong on the premises, marks on the body that suggested the use of a stun gun, and DNA samples on the girl's body. The ransom note was also suspicious. Police found that it was written with a pen and pad of paper belonging to the Ramseys. The amount demanded, $118,000, was a surprisingly small amount, considering that John Ramsey was worth more than $6 million. It is also interesting to note that Mr. Ramsey had just received a year-end bonus of $118,117.50.

A number of suspects were considered, but one by one they were cleared. Finally, the police zeroed in on the parents. For years, the Ramseys were put under intense pressure by authorities and the public alike to confess to the murder. However, a grand jury investigation ended with no indictments. In 2003, a judge ruled that an intruder had killed JonBenét. Then, in August 2006, John Mark Karr confessed, claiming that he was with the girl when she died. However, Karr's DNA did not match that found on JonBenét.

In 2008, Boulder County District Attorney Mary Lacy formally apologized to the family in a letter, saying that neither the parents nor the son were considered suspects. Lacy added that DNA evidence not available in 1996 pointed to an unknown male as the killer. The case remains unsolved.

My Bloody Valentine

During the Roaring Twenties, Al "Scarface" Capone ruled Chicago. Be it gambling, prostitution, or bootleg whiskey, Capone and his gangsters controlled it. For a few years, George "Bugs" Moran and his North Side Gang had been muscling their way into Chicago in an attempt to force Capone out. As 1929 began, rumors started to fly that Capone was planning his revenge. As the days turned into weeks and nothing happened, Moran and his men began to let their guard down. That would prove to be a fatal mistake.

GATHERING FOR THE SLAUGHTER

On February 14, 1929, six members of the North Side Gang—James Clark, Frank Gusenberg, Peter Gusenberg, Adam Heyer, Reinhart Schwimmer, and Al Weinshank—were gathered inside the SMC Cartage Company on the North Side of Chicago. With them was mechanic John May, who was not a member of the gang but had been hired to work on one of their cars. May had brought along his dog, Highball, and had tied him to the bumper of the car while he worked. Supposedly, the men were gathered at the warehouse to accept a load of bootleg whiskey. Whether that is true or not remains unclear. What is known for certain is that at approximately 10:30 A.M., two cars pulled up in front of the Clark Street entrance of the building. Four men—two dressed as police officers and two in street clothes—got out and walked into the warehouse.

MURDERERS IN DISGUISE

Once the men were inside, it is believed they announced that the warehouse was being raided and ordered everyone to line up facing the back wall. Believing the armed men were indeed police officers, all of Moran's men, along with John May, did as they were told. Suddenly, the four men began shooting, and, in a hail of shotgun fire and more than 70 submachine-gun rounds, the seven men were gunned down.

When it was over, the two men in street clothes calmly walked out of the building with their hands up, followed by the two men dressed as police officers. To any onlookers, it appeared as though there had been a shootout and police had arrived and were now arresting two men.

"NOBODY SHOT ME"

Minutes later, neighbors called police after reportedly hearing strange howls coming from inside the building. When the real police arrived, they found all seven men mortally wounded. One of the men, Frank Gusenberg, lingered long enough to respond to one question. When authorities asked who shot him, Gusenberg responded, "Nobody shot me." The only survivor was Highball the dog, whose howls first alerted people that something was wrong.

When word of the massacre hit the newswire, everyone

suspected Capone had something to do with it. Capone swore he wasn't involved, but most people believed he had orchestrated the whole thing as a way to get rid of Moran and several of his key men. There was only one problem—Bugs Moran wasn't in the warehouse at the time of the shooting. Some believe that Moran may have driven up, seen the cars out front, and, thinking it was a raid, drove away. One thing is sure: February 14, 1929, was Moran's lucky day.

Police launched a massive investigation but were unable to pin anything on Capone, although they did arrest two of his gunmen, John Scalise and Jack "Machine Gun" McGurn. Scalise never even made it to the courthouse—he was murdered before the trial began. Charges against McGurn were eventually dropped, although he was murdered seven years later, on Valentine's Day, in what appeared to be retaliation for the 1929 massacre.

AL CAPONE HAUNTED BY THE TRUTH

Publicly, Al Capone may have denied any wrongdoing, but it appears that the truth may have literally haunted him until his dying day. Beginning in 1929, Al Capone began telling several of his closest friends that James Clark, one of the men killed in the massacre, was haunting him. Several times, Capone's bodyguards heard him scream, "Get out! Leave me alone!" in the middle of the night. When they burst

into the room believing Capone was being attacked, they would always find the room empty except for Capone, who would say that Clark was after him. Some say Clark didn't rest until Capone passed away on January 25, 1947.

GHOSTS STILL LINGER

The warehouse at 2122 North Clark Street, where the bloody massacre took place, was demolished in 1967 and is now a parking lot. The wall against which the seven doomed men stood, complete with bullet holes, was dismantled brick by brick and sold at auction. A businessman bought the wall and reassembled it in the men's room of his restaurant. However, the business failed and the owner, believing the wall was cursed, tried getting rid of it to recoup his losses. He sold the individual bricks and was successful in getting rid of many of them, but they always seemed to find their way back to him. Sometimes they would show up on his doorstep along with a note describing all the misfortune the new owner had encountered after buying the brick.

At the former site of the warehouse, some people report hearing the sounds of gunfire and screams coming from the lot. People walking their dogs near the lot claim that their furry friends suddenly pull on their leashes and try to get away from the area as quickly as possible. Perhaps they sense the ghastly aura of a massacre that happened more than 90 years ago.

CHAPTER 11

STRANGE BUT TRUE

Vanished: The Lost Colony of Roanoke Island

Twenty years before England established its first successful colony in the New World, an entire village of English colonists disappeared in what would later be known as North Carolina. Did these pioneers all perish? Did Native Americans capture them? Did they join a friendly tribe? Could they have left descendants who live among us today?

TIMING IS EVERYTHING

Talk about bad timing. As far as John White was concerned, England couldn't have picked a worse time to go to war. It was November 1587, and White had just arrived in England from the New World. He intended to gather relief supplies and immediately sail back to Roanoke Island, where he had left more than 100 colonists who were running short of food. Unfortunately, the English were gearing up to fight Spain. Every seaworthy ship—including White's—was pressed into naval service. Not a one could be spared for his return voyage to America.

NOBODY HOME

When John White finally returned to North America three years later, he was dismayed to discover that the colonists he had left behind were nowhere to be found. Instead, he stumbled upon a mystery—one that has never been solved.

The village that White and company had founded in 1587 on Roanoke Island lay completely deserted. Houses had been dismantled (as if someone planned to move them), but the pieces lay in the long grass along with iron tools and farming equipment. A stout stockade made of logs stood empty.

White found no sign of his daughter Eleanor, her husband Ananias, or their daughter Virginia Dare—the first English child born in America. None of the 87 men, 17 women, and 11 children remained. No bodies or obvious grave sites offered clues to their fate. The only clues—if they were clues—that White could find were the letters CRO carved into a tree trunk and the word CROATOAN carved into a log of the abandoned fort.

NO FORWARDING ADDRESS

All White could do was hope that the colonists had been taken in by friendly natives.

Croatoan—also spelled "Croatan"—was the name of a barrier island to the south and also the name of a tribe of Native Americans that lived on that island. Unlike other area tribes, the Croatoans had been friendly to English newcomers, and one of them, Manteo, had traveled to England with earlier explorers and returned to act as interpreter for the Roanoke colony. Had the colonists, with Manteo's help, moved to

Croatoan? Were they safe among friends?

White tried to find out, but his timing was rotten once again. He had arrived on the Carolina coast as a hurricane bore down on the region. The storm hit before he could mount a search. His ship was blown past Croatoan Island and out to sea. Although the ship and crew survived the storm and made it back to England, White was stuck again. He tried repeatedly but failed to raise money for another search party.

No one has ever learned the fate of the Roanoke Island colonists, but theories as to what happened to them abound. A small sailing vessel and other boats that White had left with them were gone when he returned. It's possible that the colonists used the vessels to travel to another island or to the mainland. White had talked with others before he left about possibly moving the settlement to a more secure location inland. It's even possible that the colonists tired of waiting for White's return and tried to sail back to England. If so, they would have perished at sea. Yet there are at least a few shreds of hearsay evidence that the colonists survived in America.

RUMORS OF SURVIVORS

In 1607, Captain John Smith and company established the first successful English settlement in North America at Jamestown, Virginia. The colony's secretary, William Strachey, wrote four years later about hearing a report of four English men, two boys, and one young woman who had been sighted south of Jamestown at a settlement of the Eno tribe, where they were being used as slaves. If the report was true, who else could these English have been but Roanoke survivors?

For more than a century after the colonists' disappearance, stories emerged of gray-eyed Native Americans and English-speaking villages in North Carolina and Virginia. In 1709, an English surveyor said members of the Hatteras tribe living on North Carolina's Outer Banks—some of them with light-colored eyes—claimed to be descendants of white people. It's possible that the Hatteras were the same people that the 1587 colonists called Croatoan.

In the intervening centuries, many of the individual tribes of the region have disappeared. Some died out. Others were absorbed into larger groups such as the Tuscarora. One surviving group, the Lumbee, has also been called Croatoan. The Lumbee, who still live in North Carolina, often have Caucasian features. Could they be descendants of Roanoke colonists? Many among the Lumbee dismiss the notion as fanciful, but the tribe has long been thought to be of mixed heritage and has been speaking English so long that none among them know what language preceded it.

Ghost Ship Ahoy!

Pirates of the Caribbean movies have renewed interest in such folkloric figures as Davy Jones and The Flying Dutchman while simultaneously muddling their stories. At no time was Davy Jones captain of the famed ghost ship.

DAVY JONES

An old seafaring term for the bottom of the ocean, "Davy Jones's Locker" is the grave of all those who perish at sea. There are numerous tales about the origin of the expression, most of which attempt to identify a real Davy Jones. One version has Jones running a pub in London, where he press-ganged unwary customers into serving aboard pirate ships by drugging them and then storing them in the pub's ale cellar or locker. Other stories relate Jones to Jonah, the biblical figure who spent three days and nights trapped in the belly of a big fish.

THE FLYING DUTCHMAN

This term is often used to refer to a ghost ship that is doomed to sail the oceans forever, but it is more accurately a reference to the captain of the ghost ship. Legend holds that in 1680, Dutch captain Hendrik Van der Decken's ship was wrecked in a terrible storm off the Cape of Good Hope at the southern tip of Africa. As the ship sank, the captain's dying words were a vow to successfully round the infamous Cape even if it took him until doomsday.

Over the years, whenever there is stormy weather off the Cape, seafarers have reported seeing a phantom ship battling the waves, with a ghostly captain at the wheel. In 1939, dozens of bathers on a South African beach reported sighting a 17th-century merchant vessel off the coast and then seeing it suddenly vanish into thin air.

Truth and Myth of the Ninja

Ninjas were the special forces of feudal Japan. Trained in assassination, espionage, and guerrilla warfare, ninjas inspired fear in both rulers and commoners. The ninja has taken on a mythical status. But like most myths, the story is filled with both fact and fiction.

HUMBLE BEGINNINGS

Ninjas got their start as priests living in the mountains of Japan. Harassed by the central government and local samurai, they resorted to using *Nonuse* (the art of stealth)—what we would call guerrilla warfare. Their use of secrecy and stealth didn't win them many friends, but it secured them a role in the coming civil wars.

From roughly 794 to 1192, local rulers fought to gain control of Japan. While the samurai fought the wars, it was left to the mountain priests to do those things that the samurai considered cowardly: spying and assassinating rivals. This is when the ninja (*nin*, meaning "concealment" and *sha*, meaning "person") was born.

FROM PRIESTS TO NINJAS

The ninja made their reputation during the Japanese civil wars. They worked for anybody—and often for both sides at the same time. In addition to being scouts, a favorite ninja job was to sneak into a castle under siege and cause chaos. Dressed like the enemy, they made their way into enemy camps to set fires, start rebellions, steal flags, and generally keep the pressure on their opponents so that when the army stormed the gates, the defenders would be forced to give up without a fight.

Ninjas used weapons uniquely suited to them. They wore claws on their gloves to help them fight and climb. Because the ownership of weapons was forbidden to all but the samurai, ninjas used a common farming tool called a sickle. And, of course, they used the throwing stars that everybody sees in the movies (though the real ninjas weren't nearly as accurate as their Hollywood counterparts). They also used invisibility weapons: usually an eggshell filled with an eye irritant or a bit of gunpowder with a fuse in case they had to make a quick getaway.

Eventually the civil wars came to an end, and the ninjas found themselves out of a job. The ninjas were gone but not forgotten. The exploits of the ninja made their way into popular literature and eventually into legend.

NINJA FACT AND FICTION

The ninja were feared for their ability to assassinate their rivals, but there was never a documented case of any ruler being killed by a ninja. They tried, of course, but they were never successful.

Although ninjas are typically thought to be male, there were female ninjas as well. Whether male or female, one thing is certain: Ninjas didn't run around in black pajamas as Hollywood would have you believe.

This misconception originated in Kabuki Theater. During shows, the prop movers wore all black to shift things around while the play was going on. Everybody was supposed to ignore the people in black, pretending they were invisible. So when ninjas were played in the theater, they wore the same black dress as the prop movers to symbolize their gift of invisibility. The crowds bought it, and the black ninja suit was born.

The exploits of the ninja came to the West mainly after World War II. Like the Japanese theater, Hollywood's version of the ninja portrayed them either as an almost unbeatable mystical foe or as a clumsy fighter that the hero of the movie could take on singlehandedly.

Although there are martial arts schools that teach ninja techniques, the ninja have faded into history and legend.

Terribly Terrifying

The first all-powerful Russian ruler, Tsar Ivan the Terrible, was terrible indeed. He was terribly paranoid. It must have been his upbringing. As a child prince in Moscow, Ivan was under the thumb of *boyars* (Russian nobles). Feuding noble families such as the Shuiskis would break into young Ivan's palace, robbing, murdering, and even skinning alive one of the boy's advisors. The orphan (his mother had been poisoned) took out his frustrations on animals, poking out their eyes or tossing them off the palace roof. In 1543, at age 13, Ivan took some personal revenge, having Andrei Shuiski thrown to the dogs—literally. After other vile acts, he'd sometimes publicly repent by banging his head violently on the ground.

When his beloved wife Anastasia died in 1560 (Ivan beat his head on her coffin), the boyars refused allegiance to his young son Dmitri. Then Ivan became terrifying. He set up the *Oprichniki*, a group of handpicked thugs. After his forces sacked the city of Novgorod in 1570, he had its archbishop "sewn up in a bearskin and then hunted to death by a pack of hounds." Women and children fared no better; they were tied to sleds and sent into the freezing Volkhov River.

Over time, Ivan had the lover of his fourth wife impaled and his seventh wife drowned. Perhaps afflicted by encephalitis, and likely by syphilis, his behavior grew ever stranger. He beat up his son's wife, who then miscarried, and later beat his son Ivan to death with a royal scepter (then beat his head on the coffin).

Ivan the Terrible may well have been mad as a hatter, and by the same cause that drove 19th-century hatmakers insane—mercury poisoning. When his body was exhumed in the 1960s, his bones were found to have toxic levels of the metal.

Bermuda Triangle

The Bermuda Triangle—an infamous stretch of the Atlantic Ocean bordered by Florida, Bermuda, and Puerto

Rico—has been the location of strange disappearances throughout history. The Coast Guard does not recognize the Bermuda Triangle or the supernatural explanations for the mysterious disappearances in its midst. There are some probable explanations for the missing vessels, including hurricanes, undersea earthquakes, and magnetic fields that interfere with positioning devices. But it's tempting to wonder if the following vessels got sucked into another dimension, abducted by aliens, or simply vanished into thin air.

1. Flight 19: On December 5, 1945, five Avenger torpedo bombers left the Naval Air Station at Fort Lauderdale, Florida, with Lieutenant Charles Taylor in command of a crew of 13 student pilots. About an hour and a half into the flight, Taylor radioed the base to say that his compasses weren't working, but he figured he was somewhere over the Florida Keys. The lieutenant who received the signal told Taylor to fly north toward Miami. Although he was an experienced pilot, Taylor got horribly turned around; the more he tried to get out of the Keys, the further out to sea he and his crew traveled. As night fell, radio signals worsened, until, finally, there was nothing at all from Flight 19. A U.S. Navy investigation reported that Taylor's confusion caused the disaster, but his mother convinced them to change the official report to read that the planes went down for "causes unknown." The planes have never been recovered.

2. Flight 201: This Cessna left Fort Lauderdale on March 31, 1984, en route for Bimini Island in the Bahamas, but it never made it. Not quite midway to its destination, the plane slowed its airspeed significantly, but no radio signals were made from the plane to indicate distress. Suddenly, the plane dropped from the air into the water, completely vanishing from the radar. A woman on Bimini Island swore she saw a plane plunge into the sea about a mile offshore, but no wreckage has ever been found.

3. USS *Cyclops*: As World War I heated up, America went to battle. The *Cyclops*, commanded by Lieutenant G. W. Worley, stayed mostly on the East Coast of the U.S. until 1918, when it was sent to Brazil to refuel Allied ships. With 309 people onboard, the ship left Rio de Janeiro in February and reached Barbados in March. After that, the *Cyclops* was never heard from again. The Navy says in its official statement, "The disappearance of this ship has been one of the most baffling mysteries in the annals of the Navy, all attempts to locate her having proved unsuccessful. There were no enemy submarines in the western Atlantic at that time, and in December 1918 every effort was made to obtain from German sources information regarding the disappearance of the vessel."

4. *Star Tiger*: Captain B. W. McMillan commanded the *Star Tiger*, which was flying from England to Bermuda in January 1948. On January 30, McMillan said he expected to arrive in Bermuda at 5:00 A.M., but neither he nor any of the 31 people onboard the *Star Tiger* were ever heard from again. When the Civil Air Ministry launched a search and investigation, they learned that the SS *Troubadour* had reported seeing a low-flying aircraft halfway between Bermuda and the entrance to Delaware Bay. If that aircraft was the *Star Tiger*, it was drastically off course. The fate of the *Star Tiger* remains unknown.

5. *Star Ariel*: A Tudor IV aircraft like the *Star Tiger* left Bermuda on January 17, 1949, with 7 crew members and 13 passengers en route to Jamaica. That morning, Captain J. C. McPhee reported that the flight was going smoothly. Shortly afterward, another more cryptic message came from the captain, when he reported that he was changing his frequency; then nothing more was heard, ever. More than 60 aircraft and 13,000 men were deployed to look for the *Star Ariel*, but not a hint of wreckage was ever found.

6. The *Spray*: Joshua Slocum, the first man to sail solo around the world, would be an unlikely candidate for getting lost at sea, but it appears that's exactly what happened. In 1909, the *Spray* left the East Coast of the United States for Venezuela via the Caribbean Sea. Slocum was never heard from or seen again and was declared dead in 1924. The ship was solid and Slocum was a pro, so nobody knows what happened. Perhaps he was felled by a larger ship or maybe he was taken down by pirates. No one knows for sure that Slocum disappeared within Triangle waters, but Bermuda buffs claim Slocum's story as part of the legacy of the Devil's Triangle.

7. *Teignmouth Electron*: Who said that the Bermuda Triangle only swallows up ships and planes? Who's to say it can't make a man go mad too? Perhaps that's what happened on the *Teignmouth Electron* in 1969. The 1968 *Sunday Times* Golden Globe Race left England on October 31 and required each contestant to sail his ship solo. Donald Crowhurst was one of the entrants, but he never made it to the finish line. The *Electron* was found abandoned in the middle of the Bermuda Triangle in July 1969. Logbooks recovered from the ship reveal that Crowhurst was deceiving organizers about his position in the race and going a little nutty out there in the big blue ocean. The last entry of his log was dated June 29—it is believed that Crowhurst jumped overboard and drowned himself in the Triangle.